Judaism

A GCSE Activities Pack

Judaism

A GCSE Activities Pack

Eileen Bromley

Formerly Head of RE, Southfield School for Girls,
Kettering

To Paul.

With happy memories of
shared responsibilities!

Eileen

Jan '90.

Stanley Thornes & Hulton

First published in 1989 by:
Stanley Thornes (Publishers) Ltd
Old Station Drive
Leckhampton
CHELTENHAM GL53 0DN
England

British Library Cataloguing in Publication Data

Bromley, Eileen
    Judaism: a GCSE activities pack.
    1. Judaism
    I. Title
    296

ISBN 1-871402-02-6

Typeset by Tech-Set, Gateshead, Tyne & Wear
Printed in Great Britain at the University Printing House, Oxford

Contents

continued

Notes for Teachers

The Talmud suggests that 'Only the lesson which is enjoyed can be learned well'. This Activities Pack is offered as a tool for the teacher to promote an enjoyable as well as an informative study of Judaism.

In all GCSE syllabuses world religions play an important part. In most of them Judaism can be chosen as one of the two options. This pack should in no way be considered as a substitute for a text book. The aim of it is to encourage students to undertake their own research, using as wide a range of resources as is available to them.

It is not necessary for students to attempt all the suggested activities, indeed it would be impossible within the time allocated for such a course in most educational establishments. The coursework requirements laid down by the various examining boards differ both in length and number of assignments. It may well, therefore, be necessary to adapt the suggestions made in this pack to suit your board's requirements. One short section, A Simplified Form of Seder (Resource Sheet R4), has already been published in *The Gospels: A GCSE Activities Pack*. It is repeated here as it is obviously an intrinsic part of any course on Judaism.

As in most religions, there is a wide diversity of custom and practice within Judaism in this country, to say nothing of the situation worldwide. Of necessity a generalised picture is presented here, and not all practices included will be followed by all Jews.

The best possible way of learning about any religion is by contact with its adherents. Any contacts which can be made with a rabbi or members of a local Jewish community are therefore invaluable. An ideal situation would be to arrange a meeting between students and members of a local synagogue, with contacts continuing throughout the course. This would facilitate the discussion of various issues as they emerge. Sensitivity towards, and understanding of, another's point of view are obviously to be encouraged at all times.

The pack is divided into topics which include a variety of activities, resource sheets and worksheets. Resource sheets provide information which is necessary to complete some of the activities. There are two types of worksheets, some have space for inserting answers, others should be answered on file paper. A number of these worksheets consist of a question with stimulus material, which is divided into sections. These questions are structured and should be seen as a unit. Similarly, most of the essays in this pack are structured and students should be instructed to attempt all of the sections. Biblical quotations in the pack are taken from the Authorised Version, the Revised Standard Version and the Good News Bible.

Visits to synagogues and other relevant places should have a high priority, if they can be arranged. If it is possible to visit London, the Board of Deputies of British Jews (see address under Useful Addresses) have an excellent Jewish London Tour, including visits to old and new synagogues, a Jewish museum, a coach tour through a predominantly Jewish area and a kosher packed lunch. This is an ideal way to enjoy the flavour – literally and metaphorically – of the faith.

These activities have been designed not only to meet examination requirements, but also to encourage an understanding of, and empathy with, the Jewish community.

Bibliography

Many RE departments will be well resourced for general world religions work and the following titles have useful sections on Judaism:

A Brown, J Rankin, A Wood, *Religions* (Longman, 1988)

W O Cole, *Six Religions in the Twentieth Century* (Hulton, 1984)

C Collinson and C Miller, *Believers* (Edward Arnold, 1981)

C Collinson and C Miller, *Celebrations* (Edward Arnold, 1985)

C Collinson and C Miller, *Milestones* (Edward Arnold, 1984)

R Street, *Focus on Faiths* (Nelson, 1974)

J R S Whiting, *Religions of Man* (Stanley Thornes, 1986)

More specialised titles

V Barnett, *A Jewish Family in Britain* (Pergamon Educational Productions, 1983)

C Bryan and V Whitburn, *Shabbat* (Pergamon Educational Productions, 1985) – Living Festivals series

M Domnitz, *Judaism* (Ward Lock, 1970)

M Domnitz, *Judaism* (Wayland Press, 1986)

M Domnitz, *Thinking about Judaism* (Lutterworth, 1971)

M Gilbert, *The Jews of Hope* (Macmillan, 1984) – diary of visit to Jews in USSR

S Jameson (ed.), *The Diary of Anne Frank* (Pan, 1955)

B Kops, *Neither Your Honey Nor Your Sting* (Robson Books, 1985) – an offbeat history of the Jews

D Kossoff, *Bible Stories* (Collins, 1968)

V Leigh, *Anne Frank* (Wayland Press, 1985)

A Paraiso and J Mayled, *Soul Cakes and Shish Kebabs* (Pergamon Educational Productions, 1987) – a multi-faith cookery book

A Robinson, *The Jewish Faith and its Heroes* (Schofield and Sims, 1980)

C Roth, *New Standard Jewish Encyclopedia* (W H Allen, 1970)

The Jewish Catalogue (Jewish Education Bureau, 1973) – three volumes, American and expensive, but original, practical ideas

L Scholefield, *Passover, Chanukah, Succot and Simchat Torah* (Pergamon Educational Productions, 1982)

J Thompson, *Jewish Belief and Practice* (Edward Arnold, 1982)

R Turner, *Jewish Festivals* (Wayland Press, 1985)

A Wood, *Judaism* (Batsford, 1984) – Dictionary of World Religions series

H Wouk, *This is My God* (Fontana, 1973)

Audio-visual and Other Resources

Film and Soundstrips

Jewish Family Events – Brit Milah and Bar Mitzvah (Board of Deputies of British Jews)

The Jewish Tradition (Argus)

Festivals (Mary Glasgow Publications)

Slides

A Jewish Wedding, Sabbath in the Home, The Synagogue (The Slide Centre, 143 Chatham Road, London SW11 6SR)

Living Judaism (Council of Christians and Jews)

A Synagogue Visit (Board of Deputies of British Jews)

Cassettes

Words of Faith – Judaism (Pergamon Educational Productions) – pronunciation and explanations

Enjoy Seder at Home, Enjoy Purim at Home, Enjoy Chanukah at Home, (Pergamon Educational Productions)

Videos

Judaism through the Eyes of Jewish Children (Pergamon Educational Productions)

Jewish Festivals in a Jewish School – Sukkot (Pergamon Educational Productions)

Genocide – the Holocaust (Pergamon Educational Productions)

Posters

Rites of Passage (Pictorial Charts Educational Trust)

Jewish Festivals (Pictorial Charts Educational Trust)

Home and Synagogue (Christian Education Movement)

Other Resources

Judaica Kit and other artefacts (Jewish Education Bureau)

D Kossoff, *The Story of Esther* (record, Hallmark)

Fiddler on the Roof (record)

The Jewish wallets referred to in the text are no longer available from the Jewish Education Bureau, but individual documents mentioned may well be.

Useful Addresses

Board of Deputies of British Jews, Central Jewish Information Committee, Woburn House, Upper Woburn Place, London WC1H 0EP

The Jewish Education Bureau, 8 Westcombe Avenue, Leeds LS8 2BS

The Jewish National Fund, Harold Poster House, Kingsbury Circle, London NW9 9SP

Council of Christians and Jews, 1 Dennington Park Road, West End Lane, London NW6 1AX

Israeli Embassy, Information Department, 2 Palace Green, London W8 4QB

Israeli Government Tourist Office, 59 St James' Street, London SW1A 1LB

The Sternberg Centre for Judaism, The Manor House, 80 East End Road, London N3 2SY

Friends of Israel Educational Trust, 25 Lyndale Avenue, London NW2 2QB

Britain/Israel Public Affairs Committee (BIPAK), Information and Trade Centre, 126/134 Baker Street, London W1M 1FH

Jewish Chronicle Publications, 25 Furnival Street, London EC4A 1JT

Answers to Crossword and Wordsearch

Worksheet W27: Crossword on Jewish Festivals

Across

6 Day of Atonement
10 Anon
11 Sin
12 Me
13 Ink
14 *Lulav*
15 Air
16 Apple
17 Moses
20 Guy
22 Synagogue
25 Of
26 *Haggadah*
28 An
31 *Etrog*
33 Ram
34 *Yad*

Down

1 Ban
2 Bone
3 *Rosh Hashanah*
4 *Pesach*
5 *Menorah*
6 David
7 *Yom Kippur*
8 Ahasuerus
9 *Tishri*
18 *Shofar*
19 Esther
21 *Nun*
23 Go
24 Egg
27 Day
29 Now
30 Oil
32 To

Worksheet W36: A Wordsearch on Judaism

Adar
Ark
Bar Mitzvah
Bimah
Brit Milah
Chanukkah
Elul
Gemara

Haman
Hora
Ketuvim
Kiddushin
Kosher
Matzos
Mezuzah
Neviim

Pesach
Purim
Rabbi
Rosh Hashanah
Seder
Shavuot
Shema
Shofar

Sukkot
Synagogue
Talmud
Tenakh
Tephillin
Torah
Yad
Yom Kippur

Acknowledgements

The author and publishers are grateful to the following for permission to reproduce material:

The British distributor for Palphot Ltd (Israel) (p. 71), Southfield School for Girls and the Jewish National Fund (p. 63).

The author would like to thank the following for their help: the Board of Deputies of British Jews, the Council of Christians and Jews, the Jewish Education Bureau, the Jewish National Fund and the Israeli Embassy.

Every attempt has been made to contact copyright holders but we apologise if any have been overlooked.

Studying Judaism

For each Topic in this pack:

1 Find out as much information as possible. You will need to use as many books as you can find. Try to supplement those provided at school by enquiring at your local library.

2 Discuss any difficulties with your teacher.

3 Complete the activities and worksheets.

4 Complete any coursework suggested, in consultation with your teacher.

5 Start a file for all the work you do. Include in it the Activity Sheets (together with the answers to the questions, notes on research and coursework), the Worksheets and Resource Sheets.

6 If you have Jewish friends, discuss your work with them as you proceed. If not, try to find a way of meeting some members of the local Jewish community.

Resources

You will need the following resources to complete the Topics:
• A Bible
• As many text books and other reference books as possible
• An A4 file and file paper.

Key to Symbols

 Check

 Listen to

 Collect

 Design and make

 Discuss

 Look up, find out, research, obtain information

 Answer, head sheets, make notes, essay, write, list

 Arrange slide sequence, watch a film/video

---

 Interview, survey

 Role play, play reading, act out

 Coursework

 Revise

 Visit, attend

 Complete worksheet

 Invite a speaker

 Food

An Introduction to Judaism

Activities

 **A** Collect pictures, illustrations, articles and anything else you can find connected with Judaism. Use newspapers, magazines and travel brochures. Produce a scrapbook as you proceed with the course.

 **B** Watch any TV programmes, videos, films or film-strips that you can find on Judaism. Immerse yourself in the subject!

 **C** Make a vocabulary list of Hebrew words and add to it as you proceed with the course. Why do spellings of the same word frequently differ?

 **D** Construct a bar-graph using the information below:

Religion	Number of adherents (Estimated in 1985)
Animism	135 000 000
Buddhism, Confucianism, Shintoism, Taoism	556 000 000
Christianity	1 563 000 000
Hinduism	630 000 000
Islam	890 000 000
Judaism	15 350 000
Sikhism	16 000 000
Atheism	970 000 000

Figures from *Operation World* (WEC Publications, 1986)

 **E** Discuss the implications of the figures in **D**. Do you think that the importance of Judaism is in proportion to its numerical strength?

 **F** Complete Worksheet W1, World Distribution of Jews.

 **G** Answer the following questions:

1 In which country are there most Jews? Why is this so?

2 Only 25 per cent of the world's Jewish population lives in Israel. How would you account for this?

3 The Jewish population of Israel in 1948 was 770 000, in 1965 it was 1 900 000, in 1986 it was 3 537 000. How do you account for this increase?

4 From your general knowledge, can you describe some of the difficulties which Jews living in the USSR have encountered?

(If you have it available, see *The Jews of Hope* by M Gilbert.)

 **H** Discuss: The Jews have always been a migrant people.

Share your ideas about how and why this has been so over the centuries.

World Distribution of Jews

1 Insert the following information on to the world map above. You will need an atlas. Use an appropriate key.

Countries with over 100 000 Jewish inhabitants

USA	5 834 650
Israel	3 537 000
USSR	2 200 000
France	700 000
United Kingdom	385 000
Canada	304 000
Argentina	300 000
Brazil	175 000
South Africa	118 000

Figures from the *Jewish Year Book* (Jewish Chronicle Publications, 1987)

2 Add the cities which have more than 200 000 Jewish inhabitants:

New York	Paris
Los Angeles	Moscow
Chicago	Jerusalem
Philadelphia	Haifa
Buenos Aires	Tel Aviv-Jaffa
London	Miami

Beliefs

General

Activities

 **A** Complete Worksheet W2, The Thirteen Principles of the Jewish Faith.

 **B** Discover the hymn book of the Jews (the book of Psalms). Find and write out in your file some extracts from the Psalms which are reflected in the Principles.

 **C** Use the Thirteen Principles to describe what the Jews believe about the nature of God.

 **D** Look up the story of the Creation (Genesis 1:1–2:4). See if you can borrow slides from a photographer to illustrate this passage. Arrange a reading and slide presentation as a meditation for use in assembly.

 **E** Prepare an act of worship which could be shared by both Jews and Christians. If you have an opportunity, you could present it in an assembly.

 **F** Visit the Jewish Museum (Woburn House, Upper Woburn Place, London WC1H 0EP). Try to arrange this whilst you are studying Judaism, but it may not be possible if you live a long way from London.

 **G** Try to find a copy of the medieval Jewish hymn *Praise to the living God!* This can often be found in Christian hymn books. List the beliefs about God included in this hymn.

 **H** In a Jewish synagogue no pictures or statues of any kind are used to represent God. Discuss why this should be so.

The Thirteen Principles of the Jewish Faith

(These were formulated in the twelfth century CE by the Jewish philosopher, Moses Maimonides.)

1 I believe with perfect faith that the Creator, blessed be his name, is the Author and Guide of everything that has been created.

2 I believe that the Creator is a Unity.

3 I believe that the Creator is not a body, and that he has not any form whatsoever.

4 I believe that the Creator is the first and the last.

5 I believe that to the Creator alone it is right to pray.

6 I believe that all the words of the prophets are true.

7 I believe that the prophecy of Moses our teacher was true, and that he was the chief of the prophets.

8 I believe that the whole Law is the same that was given to Moses.

9 I believe that this Law will not be changed.

10 I believe that the Creator knows every deed of the children of men and all their thoughts.

11 I believe that the Creator rewards those that keep his commandments and punishes those that transgress them.

12 I believe in the coming of the Messiah and, though he tarry, I will wait daily for his coming.

13 I believe that there will be a resurrection of the dead at the time when it shall please the Creator, blessed be his name, and exalted be the remembrance of him for ever and ever.

From E G Parrinder, *A Book of World Religions* (Hulton Educational Publications Ltd, 1965)

Write out below the above principles which stress monotheism (the belief in and worship of *one* God).

_____

_____

_____

_____

_____

_____

_____

_____

continue overleaf if necessary

Beliefs

The *Shema*

Activities

A Study the three paragraphs of the *Shema*:

1 Deuteronomy 6:4–9

2 Deuteronomy 11:13–21

3 Numbers 15:37–41.

B Complete Worksheet W3, The *Shema*.

C Look up Deuteronomy 6:4–9 and then answer the following questions:

1 What Hebrew name is given to this passage?
2 What name is given to the objects placed on doorposts (v. 9)?
3 How do Jews carry out the command 'Teach them to your children' (v. 7)?
4 Explain how Jews keep the command in v. 8.
5 What Jewish beliefs are stated in this passage? Comment on their importance.

D Complete Worksheet W4, The *Tallith*.

E Investigate whether any Jewish aquaintances have *tephillin*, *mezuzah* or *tallith* which you could see. Inquire about how they are used. Begin some coursework on the meaning to Jews of objects, such as those mentioned above, which are used in religious observances in the home and the synagogue.

F The *tephillin* worn on the forehead has four compartments, each containing a tiny scroll with a passage written on it. The passages are: Exodus 13:1–10, 11–16, Deuteronomy 6:4–9, 11:13–21. Look up these passages and write a paragraph to explain the practice of wearing the *tephillin* and why these four passages are included inside the compartments.

G 'Shema Yisrael Adonai Eloheyne Adonai Ehad.' Answer the following questions:

1 What is the English translation of this Hebrew statement?

2 Where would you find these words written, other than on a Torah scroll?

3 When might these words be recited by a Jew?

4 Why are these words so vitally important in the Jewish faith?

The *Shema*

Deuteronomy 6:4–9

Hear, O Israel; The Lord our God is one Lord; and you shall love the Lord your God with all your heart and with all your soul, and with all your might. **And these words which I command you this day shall be upon your heart:** and you shall teach them diligently to your children, and shall talk of them when you sit in your house, and when you walk by the way, and when you lie down, and when you rise. **And you shall bind them as a sign upon your hand, and they shall be as frontlets between your eyes. And you shall write them on the doorposts of your house and on your gates.**

From the Revised Standard Version of the Bible.

The *shema* is the Jewish declaration of faith. It is the first prayer that parents teach their children as soon as they can speak. It is the last prayer of a Jew on his death-bed.

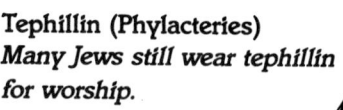

Tephillin (Phylacteries)
Many Jews still wear tephillin for worship.

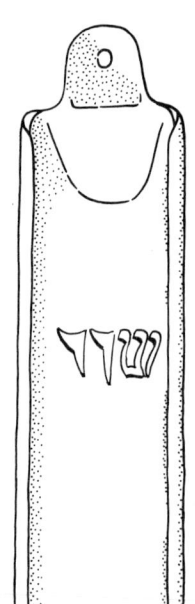

Mezuzah
Most Jews today affix a mezuzah to the doorposts of their homes.

Answer the following questions in your file:

1 What is to be found within the *tephillin* and the *mezuzah*?

2 Describe how a Jewish man or boy would put on the *tephillin*.

3 What is the purpose of this process?

The *Tallith*

Numbers 15:38–40

... Make tassels on the corners of your garments and put a blue cord on each tassel. You are to do this for all time to come. The tassels will serve as reminders, and each time you see them you will remember all my commands and obey them; then you will not turn away from me and follow your own wishes and desires. The tassels will remind you to keep all my commands, and you will belong completely to me.

From the *Good News Bible*

See also Deuteronomy 22:12

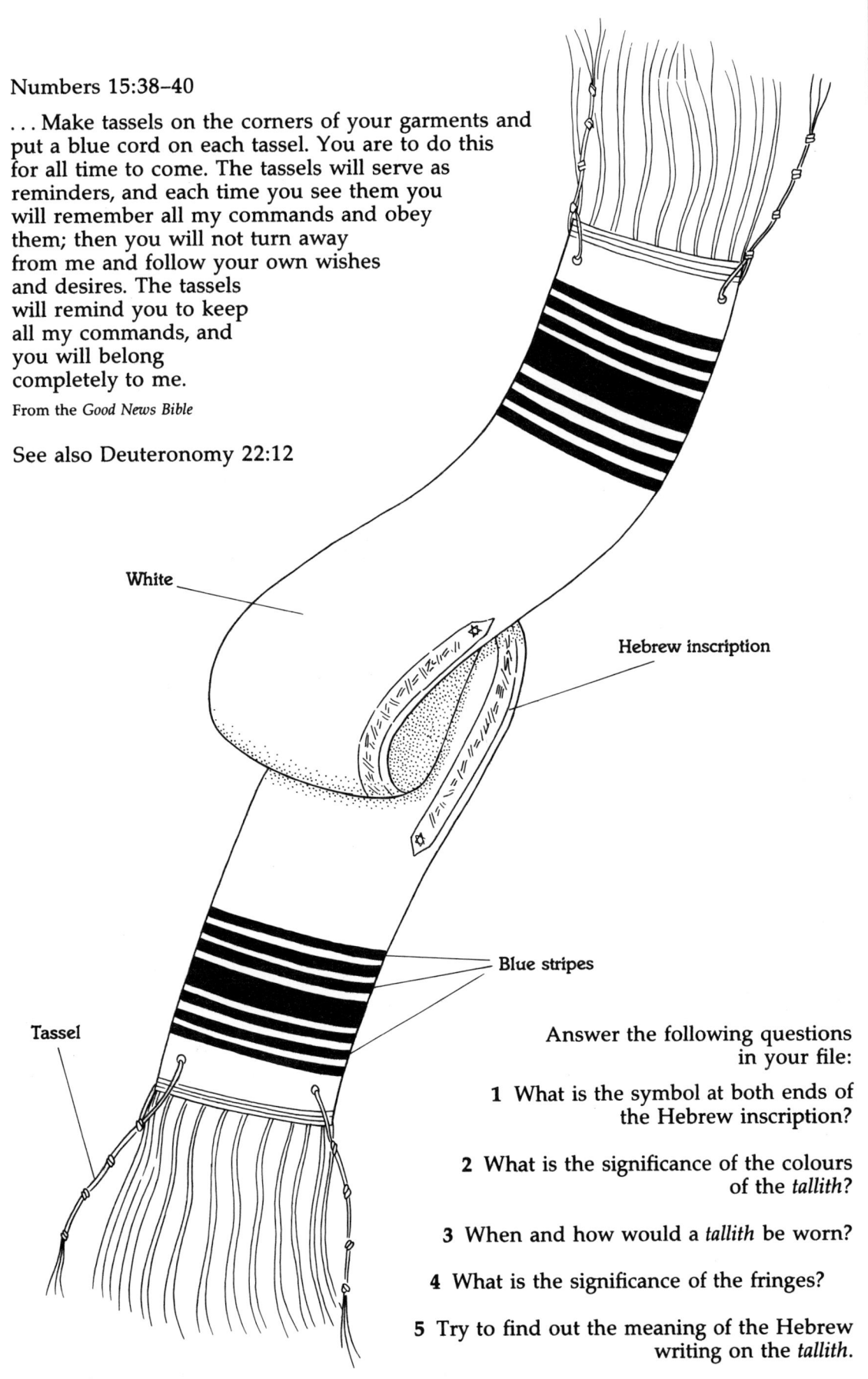

White

Hebrew inscription

Blue stripes

Tassel

Answer the following questions in your file:

1 What is the symbol at both ends of the Hebrew inscription?

2 What is the significance of the colours of the *tallith*?

3 When and how would a *tallith* be worn?

4 What is the significance of the fringes?

5 Try to find out the meaning of the Hebrew writing on the *tallith*.

Beliefs

The Covenant Relationship

Activities

A Study the following passages from the Jewish scriptures about covenants.

The covenant with Abraham –
  Genesis 17:1–8
The covenant with Isaac – Genesis 26:2–5
The covenant with Jacob –
  Genesis 28:10–22
The covenant with the nation (Mosaic covenant) – Exodus 19:1–8,
  Exodus 34:27–8
Some comments of the prophets –
  Amos 3:1–2, Hosea 11:8–9, Micah 4:1–2,
  Isaiah 49:1–7

B Answer the following questions with reference to the passages above:

1 What promises are made?

2 What are the consequences of disobedience?

3 What privileges would the people of the covenant enjoy?

4 What responsibilities would Israel have?

C Discuss: Does the political situation existing between Israel and her neighbours in any way reflect the Jewish belief in a covenant relationship?

D Look up Isaiah 41:8–10 and 42:1–7. In these passages, the chosen nation, Israel, is stated to be the Lord's servant. Make a list of the responsibilities that are laid upon Israel in these passages.

E On seeing a rainbow, the following Jewish blessing should be recited: 'Blessed art Thou, O Lord our God, King of the Universe, who remembers the covenant and who is faithful to His covenant and keeps His promise.' Look up Genesis 9:1–17. Write a paragraph to explain why this covenant, first made with Noah, is still important for Jews today.

F Head a sheet of file paper 'Blessings (*Berakhot*)'. Start the list with the blessing mentioned above and a note explaining when and how it is used. Add others as you find them later in the course.

Beliefs

The Ten Commandments

Activities

 **A** Design a poster which includes a summary of the Ten Commandments and is intended to make people read them and think about their implications.

 **B** Discuss the relevance of the Ten Commandments for people in the twentieth century.

 **C** Collect newspaper and magazine cuttings which illustrate the Ten Commandments. Display them attractively.

 **D** Interview people as to what they think about the Ten Commandments. Record the interviews if you have the necessary equipment.

 **E** Coursework: Identify what you consider to be the main problems in our society today. What relevance do the Ten Commandments have to these problems? How important do you consider the commandments to be (a) to Jews and (b) to society in general? (Use what you have learnt from the above activities to help with this coursework. See also the later work on the festival of *Shavuot*.)

 **F** Look up Leviticus 19 vv. 2, 18, 33–4. What additional moral teachings are to be found here?

 **G** Complete Worksheet W5, Question with stimulus material on the Ten Commandments.

 **H** Answer the following questions with reference to Exodus 20:1–17.

1 Which historical event is referred to in v. 2?

2 What fundamental Jewish belief is reflected in v. 3?

3 What influence have vv. 4–5 had upon synagogue design?

4 What common practices are forbidden by v. 7?

5 Why and how should the Sabbath be kept holy?

6 What is the relationship of the tenth commandment (v. 17) to the preceding ones?

 **I** Jewish young people are advised to check all behaviour against the Ten Commandments (or Ten Sayings). Discuss what changes might be necessary if you were to do this!

Question with Stimulus Material on the Ten Commandments

Answer the following questions in your file:

1 In which language would the above inscription be written?

2 Which Greek word is sometimes used to describe the Ten Commandments?

3 In which part of a synagogue would you expect to find the above object and why?

4 What do the first four commandments have in common?

5 What do the last six commandments have in common?

6 Which of the commandments do you consider to be most important for society in general today?

7 How important are the Ten Commandments in Judaism today?

8 A rabbi has said 'This unique code of codes lays down the fundamental rules of worship and of right for all time and for all men.' Comment on this statement.

Beliefs

The Messianic Hope

Activities

A Look up Worksheet B, The Thirteen Principles. According to these Principles, what is the Jewish belief about the Messiah?

B Study the following passages, which are just a few of many sections in the prophets concerning the Messianic Age:

Isaiah 2:1–4
Isaiah 11:1–9
Zechariah 14:9.

C Discuss the above passages. What do you think is being suggested about the Messianic Age?

D Answer the following questions with reference to Isaiah 2:1–4.

1 What does the word 'Messiah' mean?

2 What is meant by 'the hill of the Lord' (v. 3)?

3 Why is Jerusalem so important in connection with the Messiah?

4 What is the connection between the Messianic Age and Elijah?

5 What different ideas do various groups of Jews have about the nature of the Messiah? What is your opinion about the various ideas?

E Discuss the following suggested difference between the Jewish and Christian ideas about the Messiah. 'In Judaism, the Messianic age is more important than the Messiah . . . Christianity is Messiah-centred: it collapses without belief in Christ. In Judaism, the Messiah is God's man; in Christianity he became man's God.'

From *The Messiah in Jewish Tradition*
(Jewish Education Bureau, 1977)

F If it is possible, invite a Rabbi to speak to you on the various Jewish interpretations of the Messianic hope.

Beliefs

Other Moral and Social Laws
(including Health and Dietary Laws)

Activities

 **A** Research: Using all the books you have available, find out as many other Jewish rules for living as you can. Make a list of them.

 **B** Make a list of

1 animals that may be eaten (kosher) and

2 animals that may not be eaten (*treyfah*).

Find the information from Leviticus 11:1–30.

 **C** Look up the following references and make a note of the additional laws given here about food:

Genesis 32:25,32
Leviticus 17:14
Deuteronomy 14:21.

 **D** Coursework: You have just seen a Jewish girl looking at the menu in the canteen. She turned away and left without eating. The menu was as follows:

> Roast Pork
> or
> Sausages
> or
> Ham Salad.

Write a letter to your Headteacher expressing the reasons for your concern.

 **E** Imagine that you are a dietician working in a hospital and that you have an orthodox Jewish patient. Work out a three-course menu suitable for the patient.

 **F** Essay: Attempt all sections of this essay.

1 What is meant by 'covenant relationship'?

2 Explain the nature and importance of the Jewish dietary laws.

3 What are the main points of Jewish belief? Concentrate on beliefs about God and his relationship with his people.

4 'Be holy, because I, the Lord your God, am holy' (Leviticus 19:1). What is the importance of this to Jews?

 **G** Discuss: A Rabbi has said 'Judaism attempts to invest ordinary things with ideals and so to add a measure of holiness to the commonplace.' What evidence have you discovered of this in your study of Judaism so far?

 **H** Complete Worksheet W6, Question with stimulus material on Dietary Laws.

Question with stimulus material on Dietary Laws

Answer the following questions in your file:

1 Why are there two sinks in this Jewish home?

2 Which food law is this practice based upon?

3 Mention two other Jewish dietary laws.

4 Why is it so important for Jews to follow the laws concerning food?

5 What are the main difficulties of keeping kosher for Jews living in a non-Jewish environment?

6 'The dietary laws train us to master our appetites and not to consider eating and drinking the end of man's existence' (Moses Maimonides). What is your opinion about this comment?

Scriptures

Activities

 **A** Ask any Jewish aquaintance if they have a Hebrew scroll which they could show you.

 **B** Copy out a little Hebrew, then draw a scroll.

 **C** Read as much as you can find about the Jewish scriptures.

 **D** Complete Worksheet W7, The *Tenakh. Do not* try to learn it!

 **E** Test: Write definitions for each of the following words:

1 *Tenakh*
2 Torah
3 *Nevi'im*
4 *Ketuvim*
5 Pentateuch

6 *Mishnah*
7 *Gemara*
8 Talmud
9 *Simchat Torah*
10 *Rabbenu.*

 **F** Make a brief summary of each of the books of the Torah.

 **G** Research: Find out all you can about the celebration of *Simchat Torah*. Arrange a room like the interior of a synagogue and act out the celebration.

 **H** Enjoy some *Holishkes* – a traditional food eaten at *Simchat Torah*. Use the recipe on Resource Sheet R1.

 **I** Essay: Attempt all sections of this essay.

1 Name two parts of the *Tenakh*.

2 Describe *Simchat Torah* and explain why it is so important.

3 Explain how the Jewish scriptures are used in worship. Why do they play such an important part in the life of a Jew?

 **J** Complete Worksheet W8, Jewish Law.

 **K** Complete Worksheet W9, Question with stimulus material on the Scriptures.

The *Tenakh*

The word *Tenakh* is formed from the Hebrew initials of each of the three parts of the Hebrew scriptures: Torah, *Nevi'im* and *Ketuvim*.

Law (Torah)	Prophets (Nevi'im)	Writings (Ketuvim)
1 G_____	*A* Early Prophets	*A* Former Writings
	6 J_____	14 P_____
2 E_____	7 J_____	15 P_____
	8 S_____	16 J_____
3 L_____	9 K_____	
		B Five Scrolls
4 N_____	*B* Later Prophets	(Megillot)
	10 I_____	17 S _____
5 D_____	11 J_____	(_____)
	12 E_____	18 R_____
		(_____)
	13 Twelve Prophets	19 L _____
	H_____	(_____)
	J_____	20 E _____
	A_____	(_____)
	O_____	21 E _____
	J_____	(_____)
	M_____	
	N_____	*C* Latter Writings
	H_____	22 D _____
	Z_____	23 E _____
	H_____	N _____
	Z_____	24 C _____
	M_____	

Answer the following questions:

1 Fill in the names of each of the books. The initials have been inserted to help you.

2 Use your Old Testament to see how the 24 books of the Hebrew scriptures have been split into 39 books.

3 Each of the *Megillot* is connected with a particular festival. Fill in the name of the festivals in the appropriate brackets.

4 In your file describe how the Five Scrolls are used in the various festivals.

Recipe for *Holishkes*

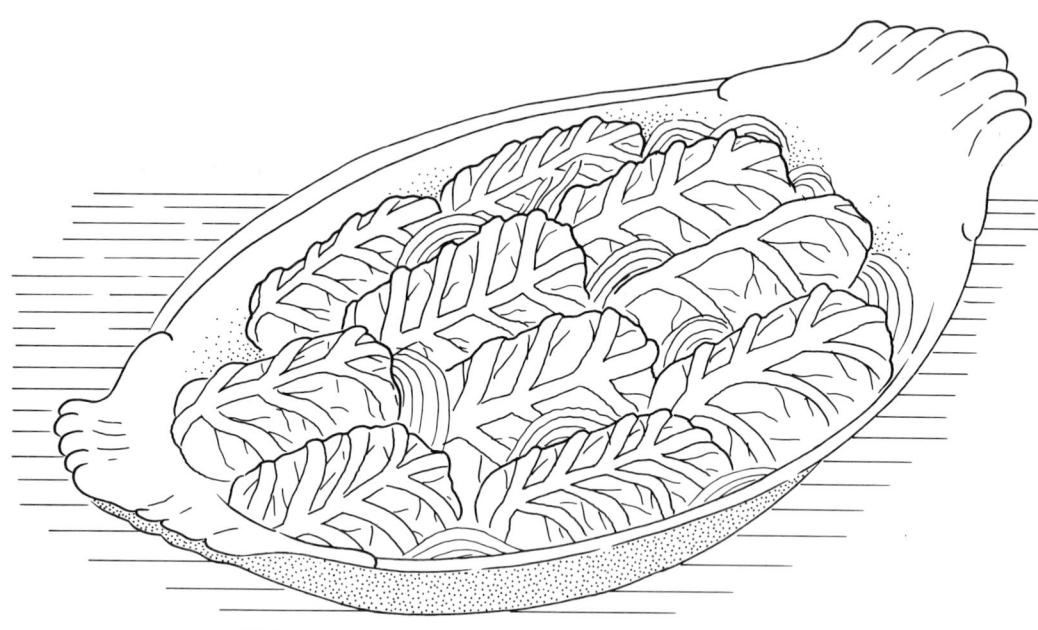

Ingredients

8–12 cabbage leaves (allow 2 per person)
1 lb minced beef
3 medium onions (2 chopped, 1 sliced)
$\frac{1}{2}$ cup long-grained rice
1 tbsp brown sugar
Oil or margarine
1 tsp vinegar or lemon juice
3 tbsp tomato paste or sauce
Salt
Black pepper
Paprika pepper
Beef or chicken stock

Serves 4–6

Method

Fry the chopped onions in oil or margarine until translucent. Add the meat and rice and cook until the meat is browned. Season with salt, black and paprika pepper. Wash and blanch the cabbage leaves (pour boiling water over them) and then remove the hard stalks. Put a portion of the mixture on to each leaf and fold it securely like a parcel. Place the cabbage rolls in a casserole dish with the sliced onion scattered between them. Cover with stock to which has been added the sugar, vinegar or lemon juice, tomato paste and a little more salt. Cook slowly for two hours at Gas Mark 4/350 °F/180 °C.

Jewish Law

The Torah

The Talmud

(32 volumes)

The *Mishnah*

The *Gemara*

The *Midrash*

Responsa

Fill in the spaces above with as much information as you can find on each topic.

Question with stimulus material on the Scriptures

Answer the following questions in your file:

1 In which language is the scroll written?

2 What name is given to the pointer? Why is it used?

3 Name two articles being worn by the reader. What is the significance of either one of them?

4 Describe briefly the contents of any one book of the Torah.

5 On which special occasions might a Jewish man be 'called up' to read the Torah?

6 Describe carefully the ceremony of taking the Torah from the Ark to the *Bimah*.

7 Why is the Torah of such vital importance to Jews? Do you consider that it is valuable for a religion to have sacred Law? Give reasons for your answer.

8 Why do you think that the Jews are often referred to as 'the people of the book'?

Synagogues

Architecture and Furnishings

Activities

 **A** Use all the books, posters and any other illustrations you have available on Judaism to find as many photographs as possible of the interior of synagogues. Identify the furnishings.

 **B** Complete Worksheet W10, Plan of an Orthodox Synagogue.

 **C** Look up Nehemiah 8:1–4. How has this passage influenced one piece of furniture in the synagogue?

 **D** Visit a synagogue if it is at all possible. See Resource Sheet R2, Visiting a Synagogue. If you are unable to make a visit to a synagogue, watch a video or film-strip on the subject.

 **E** Model: If you enjoy making things, make a model of the inside of a synagogue using cardboard boxes, matchboxes, etc. Perhaps a group could work together on this.

 **F** Discuss: History is of tremendous importance to the Jewish people. How is this evident in a synagogue?

 **G** Coursework: Following all these investigations, describe how the architecture, furnishings and symbols in a synagogue are aids to worship. Include drawings, plans or photographs and any appropriate comments made by the Rabbi or guide.

 **H** Complete Worksheet W11, Question with stimulus material on Synagogue Furnishings.

 **I** Design and produce a collage, poster or mobile of all the symbols of Judaism that you have found in your study so far. Add to it if you find more later.

 **J** 'Everything we have in the synagogue originated in the Temple.' Discuss this statement.

Plan of an Orthodox Synagogue

Gallery (A)

Downstairs seating (B)

F

Downstairs seating (B)

E

C

D G

Downstairs seating (B)

Gallery (A)

Answer the following questions:

1 Who sits at A? _____

 Who sits at B? _____

 Who sits at C? _____

2 What is the name of the cupboard marked D? _____

 What is important about its contents? _____

 _____

3 What is the name of object E? _____

 What is its purpose? _____

 _____

4 Name the object F. _____

 What does it symbolise? _____

 _____

5 What is written on object G? _____

 _____

Visiting a Synagogue

Remember

1 This is a place of worship, so behave appropriately.

2 Boys should be prepared to wear a *yarmulka* (skullcap) if requested – this is often provided.

3 Girls should be prepared to view the synagogue from the women's area, if asked to do so.

4 Your guide is there to help you. Do be prepared to ask questions. For example: How many members of the synagogue are there? How many regular worshippers? From how wide an area do they come?

5 Do not touch any of the furnishings unless invited to do so. This is especially important if you are shown the scrolls and other contents of the Ark.

6 If you have photographic equipment, ask if it is permitted to use it inside the building.

Outside

1 Are there any indications on the building that this is a place for Jewish worship?

2 Is there a notice board? Make a note of important information, e.g. the name and type of synagogue, the day and time of worship, the titles of officials. Alternatively, take a photo of it.

3 Look out for any Jewish homes (notice the *mezuzahs*) or shops (for example *kosher* butchers) in the vicinity.

Inside

1 Identify the furnishings which you would expect to find in a synagogue (see Worksheet W10).

2 Make a quick plan of the interior. Notice any differences from the plan you already have.

3 Find as many symbols of Judaism as you can and make quick sketches of them. As well as furnishings, look at any embroidery on scroll covers or parochet (curtain covering the Ark).

4 Look at a prayer book, if one is available. If it is in Hebrew and English, what do you notice about the way it is arranged?

5 If there is stained glass, make a note of its design and significance.

6 Can you work out the orientation of the building (which direction it faces)?

7 If there are any Hebrew inscriptions (e.g. above the Ark or on the windows) ask your guide what they are and make a note of them.

8 Discover whether there are other rooms in the building and what their purpose is.

In Conclusion

1 If there is time, sit quietly for a few minutes and try to absorb the atmosphere of the building. Later try to write down what you felt about it.

2 If it is possible, try to arrange a visit to experience a service of worship.

Question with stimulus material on Synagogue Furnishings

Answer the following questions in your file:

1 What is kept behind the curtains of the Ark?

2 Why is the Ark so called?

3 What Hebrew name is given to the seven-branched candlestick?

4 What symbols of Judaism are shown in the illustration?

5 Why are there no images of God in a synagogue?

6 Explain the significance of the *Ner Tamid* (everlasting light).

7 How do the objects shown in the illustration help in worship?

8 How is Jewish reverence for the Scriptures demonstrated?

Synagogues

Synagogue Worship

Activities

 **A** Attend a service of worship in a synagogue if it is at all possible.

5 Reading
6 Prayers
7 Sermon
8 *Amidah*

9 *Kaddish*
10 *Aleynu*
11 Hymn of Glory.

 **B** Watch a soundstrip or film of Jewish synagogue worship, for example, *Hear, O Israel* in the Jewish Tradition series.

 **G** Drama or mime: Arrange the furnishings in a room in a similar way to the arrangement of a synagogue. Act out the taking of the scrolls from the Ark to the *Bimah*.

 **C** Find out all you can about the three main groups within Judaism: Orthodox, Liberal and Reform.

 **H** Essay: Attempt all sections of this essay.

1 What does the word 'synagogue' mean?

D Complete Worksheet W12, Orthodox and Progressive Worship.

2 Describe three uses of the synagogue in the community.

3 How are Jews, meeting in the synagogue, reminded of the Temple?

4 Explain the religious significance of each part of the Sabbath morning service of worship in a synagogue.

 **E** Investigate the possibility of borrowing a *siddur* (prayer book) from a Jewish friend. Notice, particularly, the order of service for a Sabbath morning.

5 Why do you think that prayer plays such an important part in Jewish worship?

 **F** Write an account of a Sabbath morning service in an Orthodox synagogue using the following paragraph headings:

 **I** There is often a Biblical text written above the Ark in a synagogue. A favourite one is 'Know before whom you stand'. Discuss what this suggests about the purpose of the synagogue.

1 Psalms
2 *Shema*

3 *Amidah*
4 Taking out of scrolls

continued

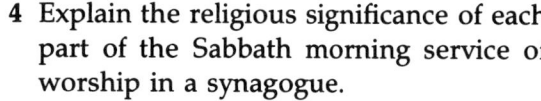
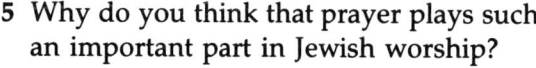

 **J** Look up Exodus 20:8–11 and then answer the following questions:

1 What does the word 'Sabbath' mean (v. 8)?

2 What reason is given to Jews for observing this day (v. 11)?

3 How are Jews told to observe this day (v. 10)?

4 How do Jews try to carry this out today?

5 Describe, and show the significance of, the end of Sabbath service in the home.

6 What do you think the Sabbath means to a Jew?

 **K** Enjoy some *cholent*, either at home or at school with the cooperation of the Home Economics department. The recipe is on Resource Sheet R3.

 **L** Complete Worksheet W13, Question with stimulus material on Synagogue Worship.

 **M** Watch the slide sequence *A Synagogue Visit*, if you have it available.

 **N** Discuss the following statements concerning the synagogue:

1 The synagogue is the outstanding religious institution in Jewish life.

2 Synagogues made possible the survival of Judaism.

3 Prayers are as acceptable in a small room where ten worshippers have gathered as in the most magnificent building.

Orthodox and Progressive Worship

	Orthodox (United, Federation, etc.)	**Progressive** (Reform and Liberal)
Length of Service	Sabbath morning (Saturday) About 2 hours +	$1\frac{1}{4}$–$1\frac{3}{4}$ hours
Times of Service	Sabbath eve, sometime before sunset Sabbath morning, about 9.00 or 10.00 a.m.	Sabbath eve, some 6–7 p.m., others 8–8.30 p.m. Sabbath morning, 10.30–11.00 a.m.
Language of Service	Hebrew Sermon and prayer for Royal Family in English	Amount of English varies from 25 to 60 per cent.
Seating	Men and women sit apart (women normally in gallery). Most members have their own seats.	Men and women sit together. No seats reserved.
Music	No instrumental music	Organ (but not in all Reform synagogues)
Officiants	Rabbi, cantor (*hazzan*) and laymen. Cantor conducts service. Rabbi preaches and sometimes reads Torah. Laymen also read Torah.	Rabbi and laymen Very few synagogues have a cantor.
Dress	Men cover heads and wear *tallith* (prayer shawl). Sometimes women are required to cover heads.	Most expect men to cover heads and wear *tallith* at morning service.

Adapted from a sheet in the *Jewish Worship Wallet* (Jewish Education Bureau, 1977)

Describe below the differences between Orthodox and Progressive Sabbath worship.

_____

_____

_____

_____

_____

_____

_____

_____

_____

_____

continue overleaf if necessary

Recipe for *Cholent*

Cholent is a complete meal which can be prepared on Friday, before the start of the Sabbath, cooked slowly overnight and eaten without any further preparation for Sabbath lunch.

Ingredients

1–1½ lb (450–675 g) brisket or thick-cut braising steak
1 can kidney beans or 8 oz (225 g) dried beans
2 medium onions, diced
3 large potatoes, peeled and quartered
½ cup of pearl barley
Water or chicken stock or soup (clear, not cream soup)
Salt and pepper

Serves 4

Method

If using dried beans, soak them overnight and then rinse them well. Put potatoes, onions, beans and barley into a large saucepan. Season and cover with water, stock or soup. Cook on a low to medium flame for one hour. Transfer contents into a large casserole, add meat and ensure that there is sufficient liquid. Cook in the oven at Gas Mark 1/275 °F/140 °C for at least eight hours. An hour or so before the meal is required, remove the casserole lid and allow most of the liquid to evaporate.

Question with stimulus material on Synagogue Worship

Answer the following questions in your file:

1 Where has the scroll been taken from?

2 Where is the scroll being taken to?

3 What do members of the congregation do as the scroll passes?

4 What is the mood of the congregation during the procession?

5 Describe a Torah scroll, explaining the significance of its coverings, etc.

6 How would you account for the great importance placed on the Torah by Jews?

7 The last sentence of the Torah is always written on a scroll so that it ends in the middle of a line. What Jewish belief does this reflect and how do Jews give expression to this belief?

Judaism in the Home

Activities

 **A** Revise the work you have done already on Judaism, noting practices which take place in the home.

 **F** Essay: 'Worship is a family matter'. Is this true of Judaism?

 **B** Describe or celebrate together

1 the eve of Sabbath ceremony in the home

2 the *Havdalah* ceremony.

 **G** Coursework: Imagine that you are a Jewish young person who has left home to go to college. What will you miss particularly in connection with your faith?

 **C** Complete Worksheet W14, Judaism in the Home.

 **H** Complete Worksheet W15, Question with stimulus material on Judaism in the Home.

 **D** Discuss: Should religion play an important part in home and family life?

 **I** Discuss the following statements about the Sabbath:

 **E** Interview a Jewish acquaintance about the place of religion in the home. Tape-record the interview if possible. Alternatively, ask a member of a local Jewish community to speak to the group on the subject.

1 The Sabbath is one of the greatest Jewish contributions to the world.

2 The Sabbath is the battery of Judaism.

3 There is no Judaism without the Sabbath.

4 The Sabbath is the royal Bride of Israel.

Judaism in the Home

This is the actual size and shape of a menorah which could be found in a Jewish home.

Explain the meaning of the following words:

Kosher _____

_____

_____

Yarmulka _____

_____

_____

Sabbath _____

_____

_____

continued

Kiddush _____
_____
_____

Challah _____
_____
_____

Havdalah _____
_____
_____

Pesach _____
_____
_____

Haggadah _____
_____
_____

Seder _____
_____
_____

Matzos _____
_____
_____

Hallel _____
_____
_____

Sukkot _____
_____
_____

Chanukkah _____
_____
_____

Question with stimulus material on Judaism in the Home

Spice-box   Candlesticks   Kiddush cup

Answer the following questions in your file:

1 Which of the above articles are used

   a) at the Friday evening celebration?

   b) at the end of Sabbath celebration?

2 By what name is the end of Sabbath celebration known? What does the name mean?

3 What is significant about the candle which is used on this occasion? How is it extinguished?

4 What is the significance of the spice-box and how is it used?

5 Do you consider that there are benefits to be obtained from observing a weekly day for rest and worship?

© Eileen Bromley and Stanley Thornes (Publishers) Ltd 1989, *Judaism: A GCSE Activities Pack*

Festivals and Fasts

Introduction

Activities

A Complete Worksheet W16, The Jewish Year.

B Discuss coincidences in the timing of festivals in any other religions you know about. Can you see any reason for them?

C Complete Worksheet W17, Jewish Festivals and Fasts, as you study each festival.

D Find a diary which includes Jewish festivals and make a list of them, with dates for the current year.

E Find a Jewish calendar. Notice that the Jewish year starts in September or October. If you live in an area with a Jewish community you may find a calendar in a Jewish bookshop or a kosher butcher's shop or even obtain one from a Jewish firm.

F A number of festivals are identified by the Jewish month in which they occur. Below is an alphabetical list of these lunar months. Find a reference book to help you list them in chronological order. Write the names of the equivalent Gregorian months opposite. Start at the beginning of the Jewish year, i.e. *Tishri – September/ October.*

Av	*Nisan*
Adar	*Shevat*
Elul	*Sivan*
Iyyar	*Tammuz*
Kislev	*Tevet*
Marchevan	*Tishri*

When you have completed the list, write the lunar months around the outside of the diagram on Worksheet W16.

G Collect any articles or illustrations that you can find about Jewish festivals from newspapers or magazines. Display them attractively.

H A blessing recited at the beginning and end of many festivals is: 'Blessed art Thou, O Lord our God, King of the Universe, who hast kept us alive and preserved us and enabled us to reach this season.' Discuss what this shows about Jewish attitudes towards festivals.

The Jewish Year

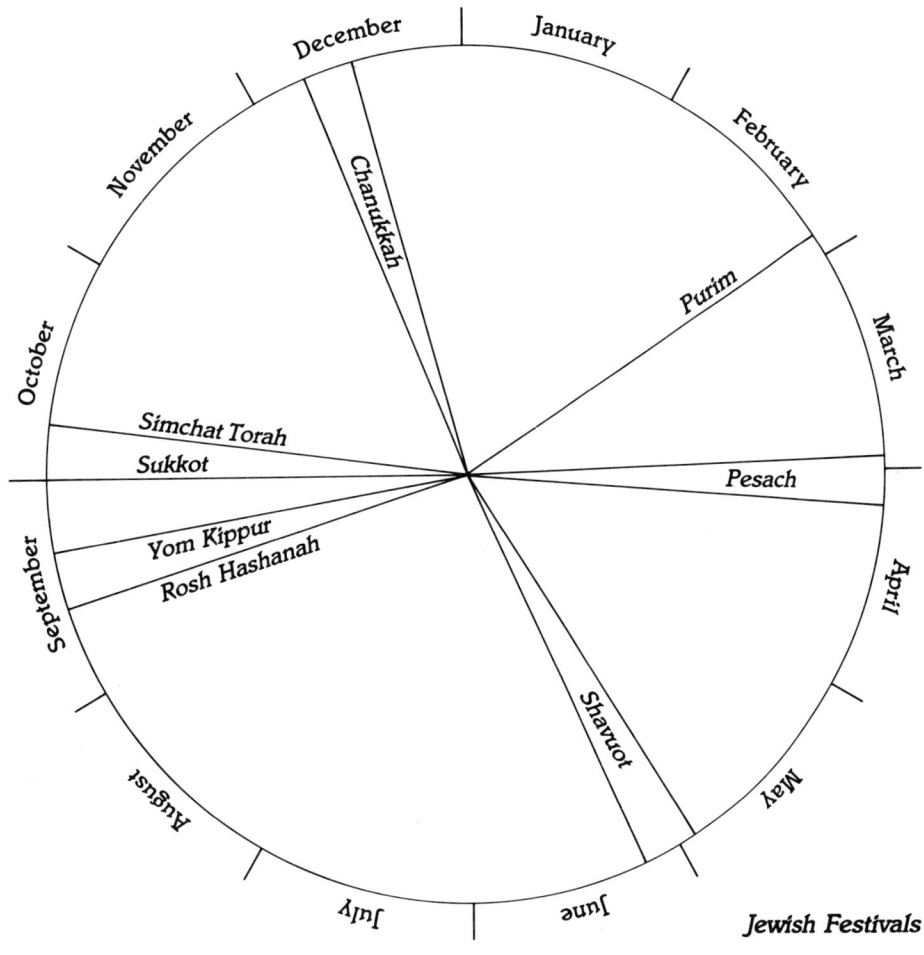

Jewish Festivals

Make notes below on any similarities you notice with the timing of Christian festivals, with a comment on the reasons for these coincidences.

_____

_____

_____

_____

_____

_____

_____

_____

Jewish Festivals and Fasts

Hebrew name	English name	When celebrated	What is celebrated	Special features
Pesach				
Shavuot				
Rosh Hashanah				
Yom Kippur				
Sukkot				
Chanukkah				
Purim				

Festivals and Fasts

Pesach

Activities

 **A** Look up Exodus 12:1–28 and make notes about the first celebration of the festival.

 **B** Watch a soundstrip, film or video of a Passover celebration if this is possible, for example, *Passover* in the Festivals series.

 **C** Complete Worksheet W18, The *Seder* Dish.

 **D** Use Resource Sheet R4, A Simplified Form of *Seder*, to experience a *Seder* service. Discuss what articles and foods you will need to produce. Consult a *Haggadah*. If possible, use a record of Jewish music.

 **E** Coursework: Most festivals have their origins in the past. As you study Jewish festivals, show how they attempt to make history come alive.

 **F** Discuss Lord Immanual Jakobovits' comment about Passover: 'On this night, we recall our past, explain our present and envision our future'.

 **G** Read Exodus 12:1–11 and then answer the following questions:

1 What name is given to the 'bread made without yeast' (v. 8)?

2 What event was this festival to commemorate?

3 How were the Israelites to celebrate this festival in the future?

4 What is the significance of the bitter herbs used in the service today?

5 What connections are there, in the modern Passover celebration, with the idea of freedom?

 **H** Enjoy some Passover food if you have not been able to arrange a celebration. Buy some *matzos*, use the recipe below for *haroseth* and try them together.

Haroseth

Mix together chopped apple, dates or raisins, nuts, a little wine or orange juice and a sprinkling of cinnamon. This is supposed to resemble mortar, so it will not look very attractive, but it tastes delicious!

 **I** Complete Worksheet W19, Question with stimulus material on the Passover.

The *Seder* Dish

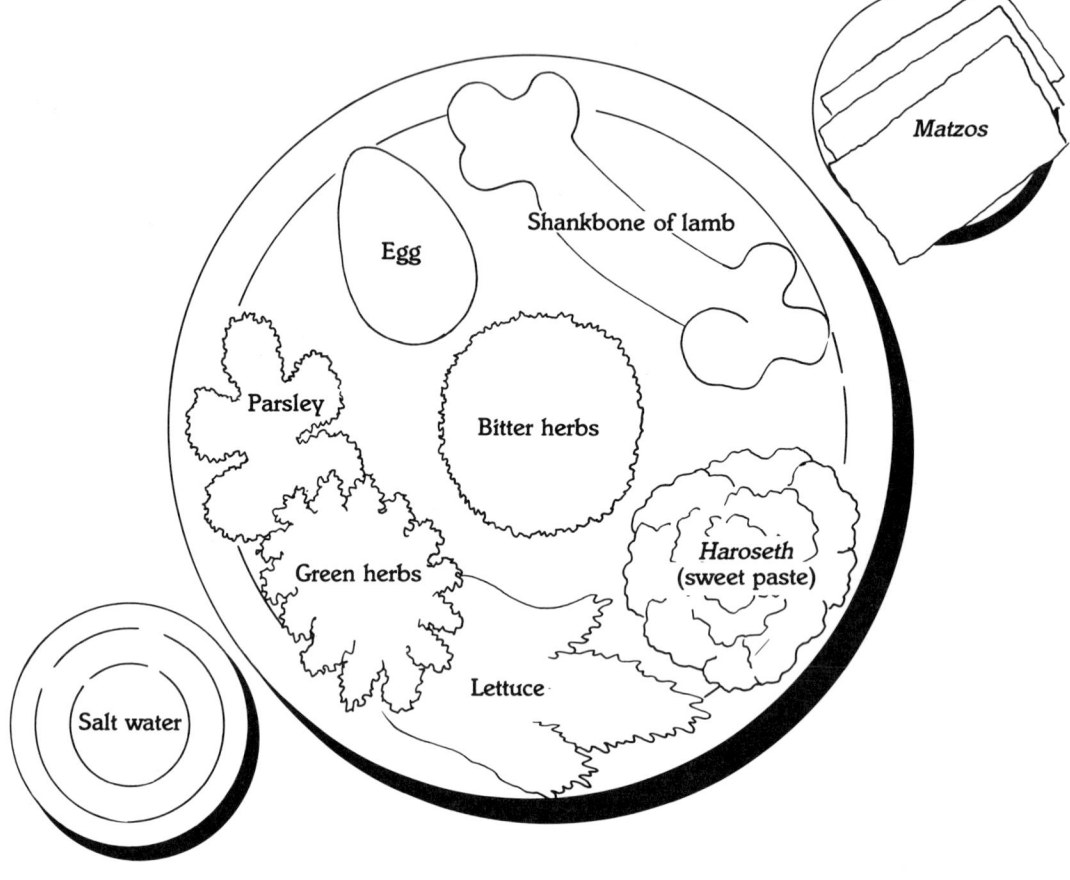

Explain the significance of each of the following:

Matzos _____

_____

Shankbone of lamb _____

_____

Bitter herbs _____

_____

Green herbs _____

_____

Haroseth _____

_____

Egg _____

_____

Salt water _____

_____

A Simplified Form of Seder

Blessing of lights (*A leader reads the script unless otherwise indicated*)
Blessed are you, O God, King of all creation, who created the stars as lamps of fire.
May the festival lights we now kindle
Inspire us to use our powers
To heal and not to harm,
To help and not to hinder,
To bless and not to curse,
To serve you, O God of freedom. *(Candles are lit)*

Blessing of wine (*All stand*)
Blessed are you, O Lord our God, King of all creation, creator of the fruit of the vine.
Blessed are you, O Lord, who chose us to be your people. You have given us times
of joy and gladness, this feast of Passover, the time of our freedom, a celebration in
memory of our escape from Egypt. Blessed are you, O Lord, who kept us safe and
brought us to this night.

Blessing of the green and bitter herbs
Blessed are you, O God, King of all creation, creator of the fruit of the earth.

Recital (*All*)
This is the bread of sorrow which our ancestors ate in the land of Egypt. Let all who
are hungry come in and eat. Let all who are in want come in and celebrate the
Passover with us. (*Matzos is broken*)

Questions (*Asked by the youngest present*)
Why is this night different from all other nights?
Why do we eat unleavened bread and bitter herbs?
Why do we dip the herbs in salt water?

Answer
We were slaves of Pharaoh in Egypt, and the Lord our God brought us forth from
there with a mighty hand and outstretched arm. And if the Holy One had not set our
fathers free from Egypt, then we, and our children, and our children's children
would still have been slaves in Egypt.

Litany (*Response by all: 'We would have thought it enough.'*)
If the Lord had brought us through the Sea of Reeds, and not led us through the
desert: 'We would . . .'
If he had led us through the desert, and not fed us with manna: 'We . . .'
If he had fed us with manna, and not given us water from the rock: 'We . . .'
If he had given us water from the rock, and not made us his own people: 'We . . .'
If he had made us his own people, and not given us the promised land: 'We . . .'

Answer (*continued*)
The memory of the escape of our forefathers from Egypt will never fail to inspire us
with new courage, and the symbols of this festival will always help to strengthen our
faith in God, the Saviour of the ill-treated. So we must learn the meaning of these
symbols:
(*Holds up lamb bone*) This lamb bone, symbol of the Passover sacrifice, reminds us
how our forefathers offered a lamb to God on the night when he led them out of
slavery in Egypt, and how they put the blood on their doorposts and were saved
from the plague which destroyed the Egyptians.
(*Leader holds up matzos*) This unleavened bread reminds us that, when our forefathers
escaped from Egypt, there was no time to wait for the yeast to make the dough rise,
so they had to carry unleavened dough with them on their journey.
(*Leader holds up the bitter herbs*) These bitter herbs remind us of the bitterness of our
forefathers' lives in Egypt, when the Egyptians treated them as slaves.
The salt water reminds us of the tears of our forefathers.

continued

(*Leader holds up charoset*) This sweet paste reminds us of the mortar used by our forefathers when they were slaves in Egypt.

(*Leader holds up the green herbs*) The green herbs are the growth of springtime and signify hope and renewal.

Each of us must enter this celebration as though *we* had escaped from Egypt: it was not only our fathers that the Holy One redeemed; he redeemed us with them. We should therefore sing praises and give thanks to him who has done all this for us. He has brought us from slavery to freedom, from sorrow to joy, from darkness to light.

Blessing of Bread (*All*)
Blessed are you, O Lord our God, King of all creation, who brings forth bread from the earth. (*Eat matzos, herbs, etc.*)
Leader Let us give thanks to the Lord our God.
All It is right to give thanks and praise. Blessed are you, O Lord our God, King of all creation, who feeds the whole world by your love and kindness. Because of your faithful care, we have enough food, and we believe that you will always provide for us.
Leader O God, the God of our forefathers, remember us as you remembered them, so that we may find freedom, grace, mercy, life and peace at this Feast.
All Amen.
Leader O give thanks to the Lord, for he is good, and his great love is without end.

Blessing of wine
Blessed are you, O Lord our God, King of all creation, creator of the fruit of the vine. (*Door is opened and a cup of wine set aside for Elijah*)

Psalm 136 (*All join in the response, 'His love is eternal'*)
Leader Shalom! Peace!
All Shalom! Peace for us – for everyone!
    Next year may all be free!
    Next year in Jerusalem!

Adapted from 'A simple form of Passover' by Sylvia Ross, as published in *Together for Holy Week*, CIO Publishing 1981. © Central Board of Finance of the Church of England. Reproduced with permission.

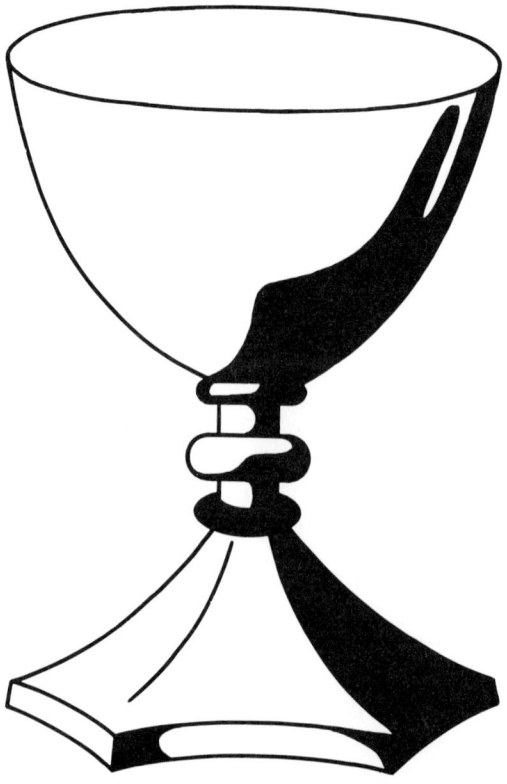

Question with stimulus material on the Passover

Answer the following questions in your file:

1 What is the Hebrew name of the festival being celebrated?

2 What name is given to the prayer book which is being used?

3 What questions are asked by the youngest child present?

4 If you were present at a similar celebration to this, and there was an opportunity to ask additional questions, are there any that you would ask?

5 In what ways could this festival be considered a festival of Spring?

6 How does the festival look both to the past and to the future?

7 Why do you think this is the most important celebration of the Jewish year?

Festivals and Fasts

Shavuot

Activities

A Look back at the work on the Ten Commandments. Notice the connections with this festival.

B Write out and illustrate the following extract from an old hymn which is used at *Shavuot:*

Could we with ink the ocean fill,
Were every blade of grass a quill;
Were the world of parchment made,
And every man a scribe by trade;
To write the love of God above
Would drain the ocean dry,
Nor would the scroll contain the whole,
Tho' stretched from sky to sky.

C Enjoy a Jewish delicacy eaten at *Shavuot.* Use the recipe on Resource Sheet R5 to make some baked cheesecake.

D Essay: Attempt all sections of this essay.

1 Explain the various names given to *Shavuot.*

2 Describe the events in Jewish history which are celebrated at this time.

3 What would the celebration of *Shavuot* mean to a Jewish family today? How would they express their faith at this festival?

E Write a full account of *Shavuot*, using the words from Resource Sheet R6 as a guide.

F Complete Worksheet W20, Question with stimulus material on *Shavuot.*

G Look up Psalm 119:97–104 and The Song of Songs 4:11. Discuss why cheesecake is a traditional food eaten at *Shavuot.*

H Look up the following passages which refer to *Shavuot*: Exodus 34:22, Leviticus 23:15–21, Deuteronomy 16:9–12. In your file, make a list of the instructions given to the Israelites about keeping this festival.

Recipe for Cheesecake

Ingredients

Base: 2 oz (50 g) margarine
           6 oz (175 g) crushed digestive biscuits
Filling: 8 oz (225 g) curd, cottage or cream cheese
           2 tbsp honey
           2 eggs, beaten
           2 oz (50 g) caster sugar
           1 oz (25 g) plain flour
           4 tbsp cream, cream substitute or top of the milk
           Few drops of vanilla essence
           1 tsp lemon juice

Serves 6–8

Method

To make the base, melt the margarine and stir in the biscuit crumbs. Press into a greased, loose-based 8–9 inch (20–22 cm) cake tin. Chill. Mix the honey and sugar in a mixing bowl and add the cheese and flour. Beat in the eggs, cream, vanilla essence and lemon juice. Pour onto the base and smooth the top. Bake for $1\frac{1}{4}$–$1\frac{1}{2}$ hours at Gas Mark 3/325 °F/160 °C until set. Leave the cheesecake to cool, in the oven with the door open, for an hour. Decorate with cream, if liked.

Shavuot

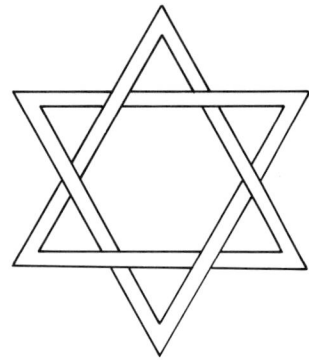

Pentecost

Feast of Weeks

Tree of Life

Deuteronomy 16:9–10

Atzeret

Feast of Harvest

Torah

Ezekiel 1

The Ten Commandments

Vigil

The Three Days of Bordering

Exodus 19–20

Ruth
Flowers
Leaves

The Day of the First Fruit Offering

Decalogue

Akdamut milin

'Could we with ink the ocean fill . . .'

Talmud

Habakkuk 3

Deuteronomy 15:19–16:17

'The grass withereth, the flower fadeth: but the word of our God shall stand for ever.'
Isaiah 40:8

Psalm 8:2 'Out of the mouth of babes and sucklings hast thou ordained strength.'

Question with stimulus material on *Shavuot*

Answer the following questions in your file:

1 Give two other names for this festival which celebrates the giving of the Ten Commandments.

2 What is the second purpose of the festival and how is the book of Ruth connected with it?

3 How and why is the synagogue decorated for the festival?

4 What is the purpose of the night-long vigil at this time?

5 A rabbi has said 'These brief ten commands ... cover the whole sphere of conduct, not only our actions but also the secret thoughts of the heart ...' What do you think of this statement?

Festivals and Fasts

Rosh Hashanah

Activities

A Design a greetings card which could be sent to a friend at *Rosh Hashanah*.

B Write a full account of *Rosh Hashanah*, having first read as much about it as you can find. Use Resource Sheet R7 as a guide for your account.

C Write a diary of the ten High Holy Days. Imagine that you are Jewish and describe how you would keep the ten days.

D Enjoy some apple and bread dipped in honey while saying the Jewish New Year greeting.

E Essay: Attempt all sections of this essay.

1 What is the meaning of *Rosh Hashanah*?

2 Give two other names used to describe this Holy Day.

3 What do Jews believe about the importance of the New Year?

4 Describe the service in a synagogue on *Rosh Hashanah*, explaining the significance of this important day.

5 What practices of the High Holy Days are meant to show the importance of penitence? Why is repentance stressed in many religions?

F Psalm 27 is sometimes read during the month of *Elul* as a preparation for the High Holy Days. Read the psalm and make notes as to how it is appropriate as a preparation for this period.

G 'Blessed art Thou, O Lord our God, King of the Universe, who hast sanctified us by Thy commandments and hast instructed us to hear the call of the *shofar*.' Look up the following references and make notes on the occasions when the *shofar* is mentioned in these scriptures: Leviticus 23:23–4, Genesis 22:13, Exodus 19:19, Joshua 6:1–5, Psalm 98:6.

H Look up Hosea 14:1–2, Isaiah 1:18 and Micah 7:19. Discuss with a partner the connection between these verses and the beliefs and practices of *Rosh Hashanah*.

I If you have an opportunity to do so, listen to the sound of a *shofar*. You may have a recording on a cassette or video, or a local rabbi may be able to help.

Rosh Hashanah

The First of the Year

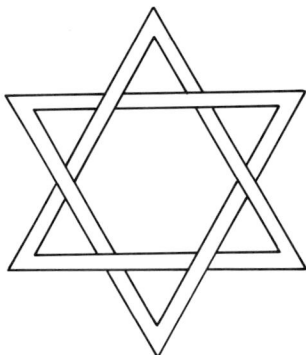

Shana Tova
A Happy New Year

New Year's Day

Shofar
Ram's horn

'The day of blowing the ram's horn' Numbers 29:1

'A memorial proclaimed with blast of trumpets' Leviticus 23:24

Day of Sounding
   Day of Remembrance
      Day of Judgement
         Birthday of the World

High Holy Days
   Ten Days of Penitence
      Days of Awe
First *Tishri*

'. . . a ram caught in a bush by its horns' Genesis 22:13

Abraham   Isaac

White robes
   White scroll covers
      New beginnings

'. . . though your sins be as scarlet
they shall be as white as snow' Isaiah 1:18

Hallah bread – *Challot* in the shape of ladders, birds or crowns

Apple   Honey

'May it be your will, O God, to give us a good and sweet year.'

Scales   Cards   Month of *Elul*

Tashlich   River   Sea   Lake   Pockets

Festivals and Fasts

Yom Kippur

Activities

A Research: Read the passages from the Jewish scriptures about the Day of Atonement, Leviticus 16 and Numbers 29:7–11.

B Complete Worksheet W21, *Yom Kippur* – a Diagram of the Tabernacle.

C Read all you can find about *Yom Kippur.*

D Interview a Jewish acquaintance about the way he or she keeps *Yom Kippur.* He or she may well help you with the diary of the High Holy Days.

E Write a full account of *Yom Kippur* using the information on Resource Sheet R8 as a guide.

F Discuss the meaning of atonement.

G Read Isaiah 57:14–58:9 and answer the following questions:

1 What is another name for the Ten High Holy Days (v. 14)?

2 'I will comfort those who mourn' (v. 18). What is the name given to the memorial service at *Yom Kippur?*

3 When do Jews fast at this time of year?

4 What, according to this passage, should be the motive for fasting?

5 How do Jews try to follow the advice of Isaiah 58:7 at *Yom Kippur?*

6 Do you think that fasting has a place in religious life in the twentieth century? What useful purposes might it serve?

H Complete Worksheet W22, Question with stimulus material on *Rosh Hashanah* and *Yom Kippur.*

Yom Kippur – a Diagram of the Tabernacle

Read Leviticus 16 and make notes around this diagram of the Tabernacle (Tent of Meeting) to show what happened in the various areas when instructions for keeping the Day of Atonement were first observed.

_____   _____
_____   _____
_____   _____
_____   _____
_____   _____
_____   _____
_____   _____

N ↑

100 cubits

Veil

50 cubits

Holy

Ark of

Holies

(or Most
Holy Place)

B

A Holy
Place

C

Laver

Altar
of
Sacrifice

Entrance

50 × 50 cubits

A = Altar of Incense

B = Table of Shrewbread

C = Menorah

_____   _____
_____   _____
_____   _____
_____   _____
_____   _____
_____   _____

Yom Kippur

Day of Atonement

The ten days of return

'Let my people return to me' Isaiah 57:14–58:14

Tenth *Tishri*

Eve of *Yom Kippur* – Meal before sunset

Covering table with white cloth and holy books

Fasting

Leviticus 16
Numbers 29:7–11

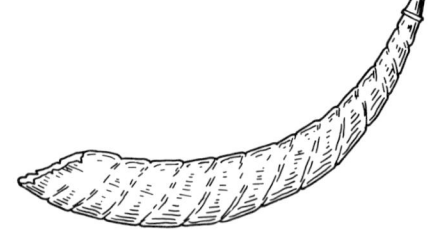

Kol Nidre

Jonah

Yizkor – Memorial service

Tzedakah – Gift to charity

Neilah – closing

Shema

'The Lord, He is God! The Lord, He is God!'

Shofar

Question with stimulus material on *Rosh Hashanah* and *Yom Kippur*

Answer the following questions in your file:

1 What are the English names of the two special days in the Jewish calendar when the above activity could be seen in a synagogue?

2 What is important about the colour of the officiant's robes?

3 What Hebrew name is given to the ram's horn?

4 What is the importance of the month of *Elul* before the High Holy Days?

5 The *Midrash* says 'When a man sins during the year the record of his transgression is inscribed in faint ink. If he repents during the Ten Days of Penitence the record is erased. If not, it is written in indelible ink.' What does this suggest about Jewish beliefs concerning repentance and forgiveness?

Festivals and Fasts

Sukkot

Activities

A Research: Read Leviticus 23:39–43 to discover how this festival was kept centuries ago.

G Complete Worksheet W23, Question with stimulus material on *Sukkot*.

B Discuss the various historical events and ideas about God that are remembered at this festival.

H Refer back to your work on the Scriptures in Topic 4 and revise what you discovered then about *Simchat Torah*. What is the connection between *Sukkot* and *Simchat Torah*?

C Write a full account of *Sukkot* using the information on Resource Sheet R9 as a guide.

I *Sukkot* is one of the three pilgrim festivals. Look up Deuteronomy 16:16–17 and answer the following questions:

1 What were the other two pilgrim festivals?

2 Where did Jews go to on these pilgrimages?

3 What were the purposes of such pilgrimages?

D Arrange a Harvest Thanksgiving. If this work is being done in the Autumn, arrange a celebration which includes various customs of *Sukkot*.

E Construct a model of, or an actual *sukkah*. Remember the comment, 'We may look up at the stars and direct our thoughts towards God.'

J Look up Zechariah 14 vv. 6–9, 16–17 and try to find out how these verses are reflected in customs associated with *Sukkot*.

F Discuss how *Sukkot* commemorates the protection given to the Israelites during their wanderings through the desert after the exodus.

K If it is possible, watch the video *Jewish Festivals in a Jewish School* – Sukkot.

Sukkot

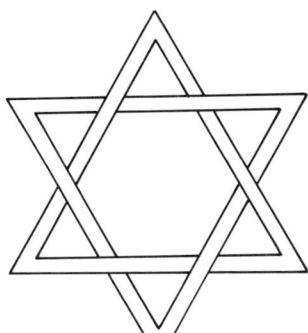

Festival of Tabernacles

Booths

Sukkah

Ingathering

Harvest Festival

'You shall dwell in booths for seven days.' Leviticus 23:42

'Blessed art thou, O Lord our God . . . who has commanded us to dwell in the tabernacle.'

Wilderness

40 Years

Moses

Pomegranates

  Apples

    Oranges

      Grapes

        Tomatoes

          Sweetcorn

        Sweets

        Flour

      Oil

    Water

Guests: Abraham   Isaac

             Jacob   Joseph

             Moses   Aaron

                    David

God's presence
and care

North	South	East	West

Four elements:

Fire	Earth	Water	Air
Etrog – Citron	Myrtle	Willow	Palm branches – *lulav*

Question with stimulus material on *Sukkot*

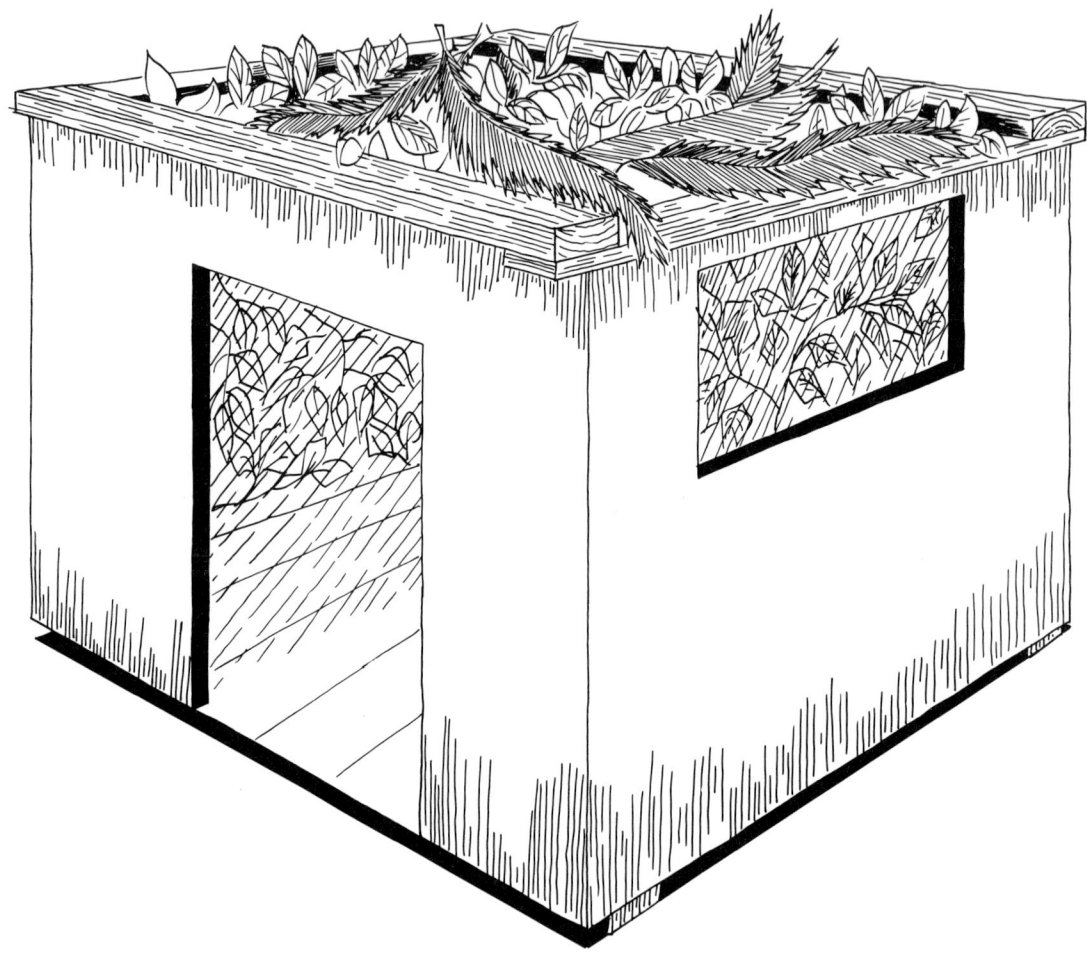

Answer the following questions in your file:

1 What name is given to this construction?

2 Describe the decoration.

3 Name four of the seven fruits that are often hung from the roof of this structure.

4 Give two other names for this festival.

5 Which event, recorded in the Scriptures, is celebrated at this time?

6 What are the four symbols used at this festival and what do they represent?

7 What would the celebrations in the home at this festival mean to a Jew?

8 How is the importance of hospitality emphasised at this festival?

9 What idea about God does the waving of the *lulav* demonstrate?

10 'The *sukkah* emphasises the transience of life'. What do you think this statement means?

Festivals and Fasts

Chanukkah

Activities

 **A** Research: Try to obtain a copy of the Apocrypha and read the story on which this festival is based from the books of Maccabees.

 **G** Design an appropriate *menorah* for *Chanukkah*.

 **B** Drama: Mime or act the story of Antiochus, Mattathias and Judas.

 **H** Discuss the importance of light as a symbol in various religions that you know about.

 **C** Write an account of the festival of *Chanukkah* using the information on Resource Sheet R10 as a guide.

 **I** Design and make a *Chanukkah* greetings card.

 **D** Find out what is remembered on each of the eight days of *Chanukkah* as the candles are lit.

 **J** Complete Worksheet W24, Question with stimulus material on *Chanukkah*.

 **E** Enjoy some traditional food – *latkes* and/or *dreidel* cakes. Use the recipe on Resource Sheet R11.

 **K** *Chanukkah* means dedication. Discuss: Is this name appropriate for the festival?

 **F** Make a *dreidel* and play the *dreidel* game.

 **L** On the first night of *Chanukkah*, a flame is lit at Modi'in in Israel, and runners take torches to Jerusalem and Tel Aviv. Try to find out why this happens.

Chanukkah

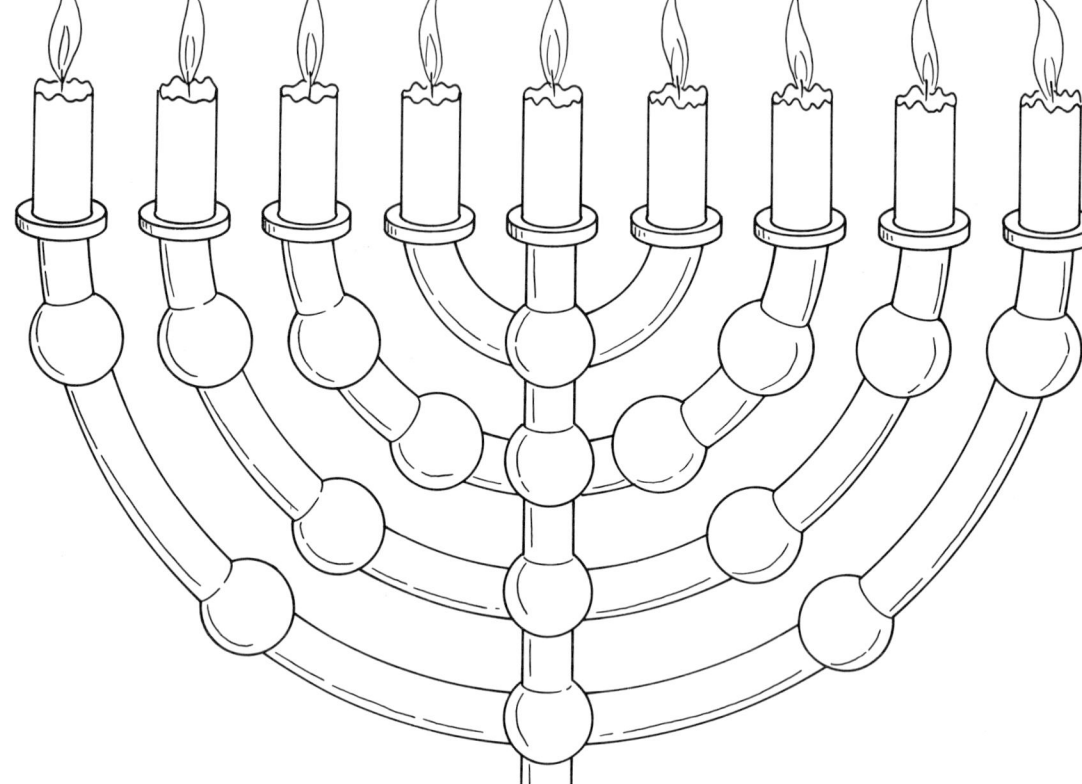

Festival of Lights

Maccabees I & II

Mattathias

Chanukkah - Dedication

Eight days

Antiochus Epiphanes

171 BCE

Apocrypha

One day's supply of oil

Menorah

Shammash

Dreidel

Latkes

Judas Maccabeus

Eight days

Talmud

Joy   *Parties*   *Presents*   *Freedom*

'Not by might, nor by power, but by my Spirit, says the Lord of hosts.' Zechariah 4:6

Recipe for *Dreidel* Cakes

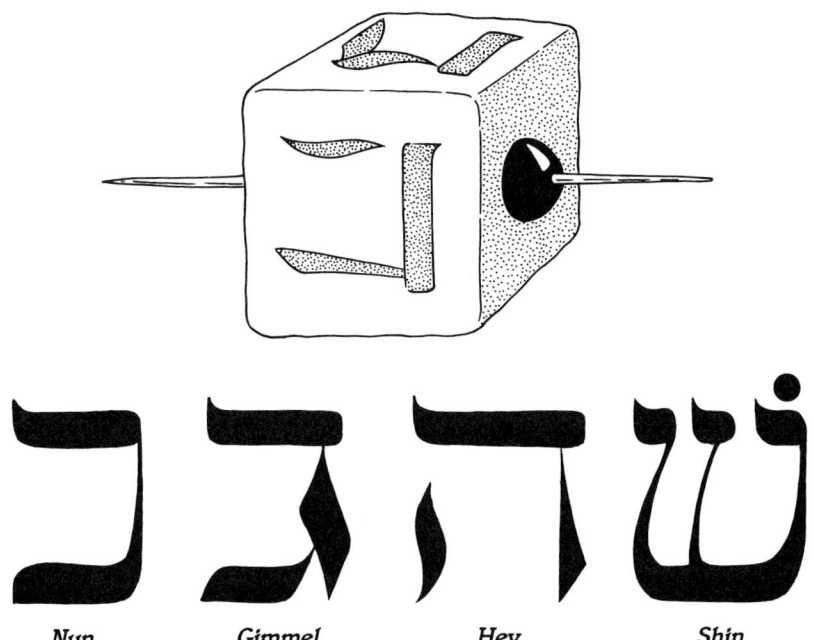

Nun   Gimmel   Hey   Shin

Ingredients

Cake mixture:
5 oz (150 g) margarine
5 oz (150 g) sugar
6 oz (175 g) self-raising flour
2 or 3 eggs (depending on size)
1 tsp lemon juice
Pinch of salt

Icing:
1 lb (450 g) icing sugar
2 tbsp lemon juice
A little yellow and green colouring
Cherries to decorate
Cocktail sticks

Makes at least a dozen cakes

Method

Cream margarine and sugar. Add the beaten eggs slowly, alternately with a little flour. Mix in the remaining flour, salt and lemon juice. Put the mixture into a greased, shallow, square or oblong baking tin and bake at Gas Mark 4/350 °F/ 180 °C for 20–25 minutes. Leave to cool completely and then cut into squares.

To make the icing, gradually add lemon juice to sieved icing sugar. While still quite stiff, leave a little on one side for decoration. Add one or two drops of yellow colouring to the remainder and coat the cakes with this lemon glacé icing. Put a cocktail stick through each cake. Add a drop of green colouring to the reserved, stiffer, icing. When the coating has set, pipe the green icing onto the four sides of each cake in the shape of the Hebrew letters shown above. Add half a cherry to each stick.

Question with stimulus material on *Chanukkah*

Answer the following questions in your file:

1 Give another name for this festival.

2 What do we call the nine-branched candlestick?

3 What name is given to the central candle from which the other eight candles are lit?

4 Why is it a common tradition to eat fried food at this festival?

5 Why is this a minor festival?

6 How does this festival bring to life an event from Jewish history?

7 Why does light play such an important part in this festival? How would you account for the importance of light as a symbol in various religions?

Festivals and Fasts

Purim

Activities

A Research: Discover all you can about the story on which this festival is based, from the book of Esther.

B Drama: Mime or act the story.

C Listen to a record, or read the story of Esther as told by David Kossoff in his *Bible Stories.*

D Write an account of *Purim* using information on Resource Sheet R12 as a guide.

E Design some appropriate masks which might be used in presenting the story of Esther.

F Enjoy some *Hamantashen* (Haman's ears). Use the recipe on Resource Sheet R13.

G Answer the following questions, using Esther 9:20–23.

1 What name is given to the holiday in the month of *Adar*?

2 What were 'these events' (v. 20)?

3 Why is this festival sometimes called Lots?

4 What is a gregger and how is it used in this celebration?

5 This festival is especially enjoyed by Jewish children. Why is this so?

6 What connection is there between this festival and the idea of freedom? In which other festivals is freedom emphasised?

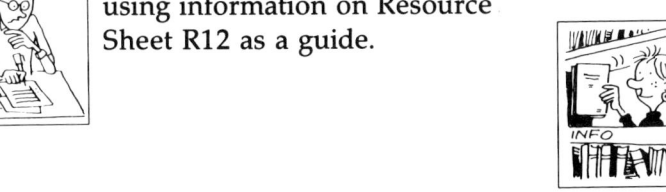

H Find out about *hora*-dancing. Could you attempt a demonstration?

I Read Esther 4 and discuss why some Jews observe the day before *Purim* as a fast day.

J Sometimes posters are displayed at this festival which say: Be happy. It's *Adar*. Design a poster with these words on it.

Purim

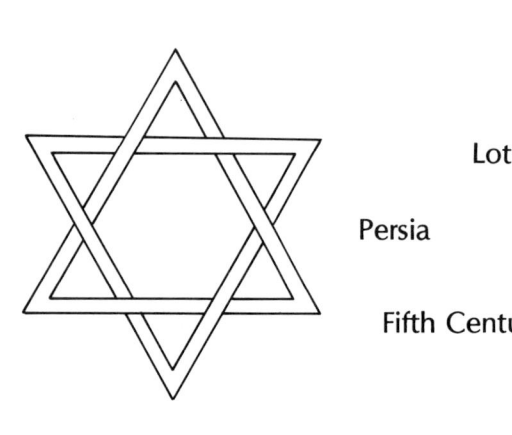

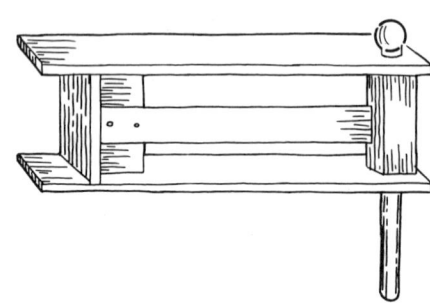

Lots

Persia

Fifth Century BCE

Gregger

Rattle

Booing

Susa

Cheering

'Haman sought to destroy all the Jews . . . throughout the whole Kingdom.' Esther 3:6

Ahasuerus – Xerxes I

Spring

Adar fourteenth and fifteenth

Esther

Mordecai

Gifts for the poor

Kreplach

Haman

Parties

Hamantashen

Fancy dress

Plays

Carnivals

Floats

Games

Hora-dancing

Fireworks

'Today is *Purim*
Tomorrow no more.
Give me a penny,
I'll be gone from your door.'

'Guys'

'All the city of Susa shouted for joy. For the Jews there was light and joy, gladness and honour . . . feasting and holiday.' Esther 8:15–17

'Blessed art thou, O Lord our God . . . who wrought miracles for our fathers in days of old at this season.'

Recipe for *Hamantaschen*

Ingredients

Sweet Pastry:
6 oz (175 g) plain flour
4 oz (100 g) self-raising flour
4 oz (100 g) margarine
4 oz (100 g) caster sugar
2 egg yolks
$\frac{1}{4}$ tsp cinnamon

Filling:
2 oz (50 g) raisins
2 oz (50 g) currants
2 oz (50 g) sultanas
1 oz (25 g) mixed peel
1 cooking apple, peeled and chopped
2 oz (50 g) caster or brown sugar
Orange juice or juice and rind of 1 lemon
Milk or egg white and a little caster sugar for glaze

Serves at least a dozen people.

Method

To make the pastry, first sieve the flours and cinnamon. Rub in the fat and add the sugar. Use the egg yolks to mix to a dough. Knead and roll out. Cut into rounds using either a large cutter or a small saucer.

To make the filling, mix the dry ingredients, apple and lemon rind (if used), then add sufficient fruit juice to bind the mixture together. Put a teaspoonful of the filling in the centre of each pastry round. Moisten the edges of the pastry and draw them together to make a somewhat rounded pyramid. Place on a baking sheet, glaze with milk or egg white and sprinkle with caster sugar. Bake at Gas Mark 6/400 °F/200 °C for 25–30 minutes.

Festivals and Fasts

Tu b'Shevat

Activities

 **A** Find out the significance of the planting of (a) a cedar tree and (b) a cypress tree in ancient Israel. To what use were the grown trees put?

 **B** Research: Make a list of the 15 fruits once eaten at this festival. Use a concordance to discover which of these fruits are mentioned in the Jewish scriptures. Look up the passages and read them. If you are able to obtain them, eat the fruit, following the practice at Tu b'Shevat!

 **C** Discuss: 'The Israelites were the first conservationists'. Read Deuteronomy 20:19–20 and discuss this.

 **D** Talk about the fact that 6 000 000 trees have been planted in one area of Israel as a memorial to the victims of the Holocaust. Do you think this is an appropriate memorial?

 **E** Revise: 'Blessed are you, O Lord our God, King of the Universe, who creates the fruit of the tree'. Look up the blessings used at other Jewish festivals.

 **F** Complete Worksheet W25, Question with stimulus material on the New Year for Trees.

 **G** Find out how *Tu b' Shevat* is a festival of Spring.

 **H** Look up the following passages and make notes about their connections with this festival:

Genesis 1:11–2, 2:9
Leviticus 19:23–5
Isaiah 41:19
Ezekiel 17:22–4, 36:34–6.

Question with stimulus material on the New Year for Trees

Answer the following questions in your file:

1 What name is given to the tree-planting ceremony held on the fifteenth of *Shevat*?

2 Why is this festival held at this time of year?

3 Which tree is the first to come into blossom in Israel?

4 Why is this festival sometimes known as Arbour Day?

5 How might Jews celebrate this festival

  a in Israel?

  b in other parts of the world?

6 What aspects of conservation are featured in this festival?

7 Explain why afforestation is so important in the modern state of Israel.

8 'In the future, each man will have to give account of having seen wonderful foods – and not having eaten them' (Talmud). Explain the significance of these words, which are often quoted at this festival.

Festivals and Fasts

Tish b'Av

Activities

A Read and make notes on 2 Kings 25:1–12, which describes the destruction of the first temple in 586 BCE.

B Read the Book of Lamentations.

C Discuss why you think Lamentations is read at *Tish b'Av*. Do you notice any suggestion of hope and restoration?

D Research: Refer to the information on Resource Sheet R14. Using all the reference books you have available, discover more about the Fast of Av. Make this a group activity and share information as you discover it.

E Essay: Attempt all sections of this essay. The word 'remember' appears approximately 168 times in the Jewish scriptures. It has been suggested that this word is the clue to the identity and survival of the Jews.

1 What are Jews remembering at *Tish b'Av*?

2 Choose two other Jewish festivals and explain what is being remembered.

3 What is meant by the suggestion that the word 'remember' is the clue to the survival of the Jews?

4 Do you think it is desirable to remember times of national and personal suffering? Give reasons for your opinions.

F Try to find a copy of the Works of Josephus in a library and read about the destruction of the second Temple in 70 CE. You will find this information in *Wars of the Jews,* book 6, chapters 4–5.

G Test yourself by answering the following questions (without looking at Resource Sheet R14!):

1 On what date is this festival celebrated?

2 What will have happened during the previous nine days?

3 Why is *Tish b'Av* a fast day?

4 What event of 586 BCE is remembered?

5 What event of 70 CE is remembered?

6 What happened in 1492 CE which is also remembered?

7 Why are low stools used for seating in some synagogues?

8 Why is Lamentations read?

9 What is *kinnot*?

10 What is worn for the afternoon service, contrary to normal practice?

Tish b'Av

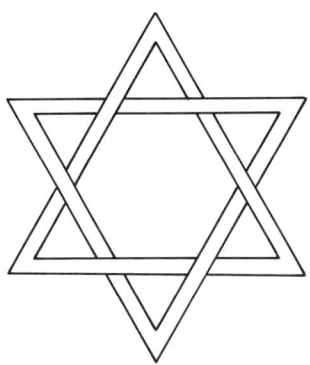

Ninth *Av*

Temple ruins

Talmud

Disasters and Tragedies
        586 BCE – Destruction of first Temple
         70 CE – Destruction of second Temple – ninth *Av*
        1492 CE – Expulsion from Spain

Previous nine days – Self denial
                        No meat?
                       No wine?
                      No shaving?
                       No new clothes?
                        No entertainment?

25-hour fast

                        Memorial lamps for Jewish martyrs

Synagogue: Evening – No *parochet*
                        No leather shoes
                       Low stools
                        Candlelight
                         Lamentations
                          Book of Job

            Morning – *Kinnot* – Dirge
                        Deuteronomy 4:25–40
                        Jeremiah 8:13–9:23

            Afternoon – Torah reading – Exodus 32:11–14 and 34:1–10
                        Tallith and *Tephillin*

Festivals and Fasts

Revision

Activities

 **A** Check that you have completed Worksheet W17, Jewish Festivals and Fasts.

 **B** Complete Worksheet W26, Short Answer Test on Jewish Festivals.

 **C** Complete Worksheet W27, Crossword on Jewish Festivals.

 **D** Essay: Attempt all sections of this essay.

1 Name four important festivals other than *Pesach* which are celebrated by Jews.

2 Describe how two of these festivals are celebrated.

3 What connections are there between the festivals you have described and Jewish history?

4 Why does the annual cycle of festivals and fasts play such an important part in Judaism?

5 Judaism has more festivals than most other religions. What religious benefits do you see in this for Jews?

 **E** In recent times some Jewish communities have added two additional festivals to the traditional ones. Find out as much as you can about each of them and make notes in your file:

1 *Yom ha-Shoah* (Day of the Holocaust)
2 *Yom ha-Azmaut* (Independence Day in Israel).

 **F** Imagine that you have the opportunity to put questions about Jewish festivals to a Rabbi. Make a list of questions that you would like to have answered. If it is not possible to put these questions to a Jewish person, try to find the answers elsewhere.

 **G** If it is possible, invite a Rabbi or a member of a Jewish congregation to speak about Jewish festivals in general, or about one particular festival.

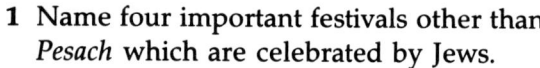

 **H** Imagine that you have an invitation to visit a Jewish family for any festival of your choice. Which one will you choose and why? Discuss your choices.

 **I** Write a letter to the Jewish family and give reasons for the choice you have made.

Short Answer Test on Jewish Festivals

Answer the following questions:

1 What is *Tishri?* _____

2 What is the Hebrew word for Passover? _____

3 What is *Rosh Hashanah?* _____

_____

4 What is the Hebrew name for tabernacles? _____

5 What is *haroseth?* _____

_____

6 Why is an extra place set at the *seder* table? _____

_____

7 What is celebrated at *Shavuot?* _____

_____

_____

8 When and why is the *shofar* used? _____

_____

9 What event is remembered at *Chanukkah?* _____

_____

_____

10 What is commemorated at *Purim?* _____

_____

_____

11 Which words from Isaiah 1 are quoted at *Yom Kippur?* _____

_____

12 Name the four symbols associated with the four elements at *Sukkot.* _____

_____

Crossword on Jewish Festivals

CLUES

Across

6 *Yom Kippur.* (3.2.9)
10 Unknown. (4)
11 Cast off during *tashlich*. (3)
12 'Let my people return to _____ .' (2)
13 'Could we with _____ the ocean fill . . .' (3)
14 Palm branches. (5)
15 One of the four elements. (3)
16 Dipped in honey at New Year. (5)
17 Remembered at *Shavuot.* (5)
20 May be burnt at *Purim.* (3)
22 A *sukkah* may be built here. (9)
25 Ten days _____ return. (2)
26 The Passover prayer book. (8)
28 _____ egg on the *seder* dish. (2)
31 Citron. (5)
33 The horn becomes a trumpet. (3)
34 Used as a pointer. (3)

Down

1 A fast is a _____ on food. (3)
2 From the shank of a lamb. (4)
3 New Year. (4.8)
4 Passover. (6)
5 Could be seven- or eight-branched. (7)
6 A 'guest' at *Sukkot.* (5)
7 The day for repentance and fasting. (3.6)
8 The King who is remembered at *Purim.* (9)
9 *Rosh Hashanah* is on first _____ . (6)
18 Blown in the synagogue. (6)
19 She is remembered at *Purim.* (6)
21 A Hebrew letter. (3)
23 'Let my people _____ '. (2)
24 A roasted one is used at Passover. (3)
27 _____ of Judgement. (3)
29 Present. (3)
30 Miraculously supplied at *Chanukkah.* (3)
32 Haman sought _____ destroy all the Jews. (2)

Rites of Passage

Brit Milah

Activities

A Use any books you have available to find out as much as possible about the ceremony of circumcision.

B Find out what happens in the synagogue following the birth of a girl.

C Research: Read Exodus 13:1–2, 11–16. Discover what you can about the practice of the redemption of the first-born today.

D Read Genesis 17:1–14 and then answer the following questions:

1 What Hebrew words describe this ceremony?

2 What is a covenant? What other covenants are important to Jews?

3 Are there any circumstances in which this ceremony is not carried out on the eighth day?

4 What happens today to celebrate the birth of a daughter?

5 Circumcision is still carried out, nearly 4000 years after the time of Abraham. What does this suggest to you about the importance of religious practices to Jews?

E 'Blessed art Thou, O Lord our God, King of the Universe, who hast sanctified us by Thy commandments and hast commanded us to make our sons enter into the covenant of Abraham our Father.' Answer the following questions:

1 At which ceremony are these words spoken?

2 Who recites this blessing?

3 What part is played in this ceremony by
a the *Sandek*?
b the *Mohel*?

4 What is the meaning of 'who hast sanctified us by Thy commandments'?

5 At what point in the ceremony is the child named?

6 How and why is wine used at this ceremony?

7 What does the ceremony mean to a Jewish family?

8 Do you consider that it is important to have a religious ceremony connected with the birth of a child? Give reasons for your opinions.

F If it is possible, watch the section on *Brit Milah* from the filmstrip *Jewish Family Events – Brit Milah and Bar Mitzvah*.

Rites of Passage

Bar Mitzvah

Activities

A Coursework: Trace the importance of religious ceremonies in the life of a Jew, from birth to death. Use photographs, illustrations or newspaper cuttings to illustrate your work.

B Interview a Jewish acquaintance about the meaning of the *Bar Mitzvah* ceremony to him. If this is not possible, try to watch a film, soundstrip or video of a *Bar Mitzvah*.

C Look out for *Bar Mitzvah* cards in stationers in large towns. Design an appropriate one yourself.

D Find out about *Bat Mitzvah* – the ceremony for girls in some synagogues. What are the differences between this ceremony and *Bar Mitzvah*?

E If you have the *Lifetime of a Jew* wallet available, study the Certificate of *Bar Mitzvah* and answer these questions:

1 Which language, other than English, appears on the certificate?

2 What is the decoration on the right of the certificate? Why do you think this has been used?

3 Explain the meaning of the words 'called to the Torah'.

4 What is the significance of the *Bar Mitzvah* ceremony for a Jewish boy? How has his upbringing prepared him for this ceremony?

F Complete Worksheet W28, Question with stimulus material on *Bar Mitzvah*.

Question with stimulus material on *Bar Mitzvah*

ברכות לבר המצוה
BAR MİTZVA WİSHES

Answer the following questions in your file:

1 At what age would a Jewish boy receive a card like the one illustrated?

2 What does the illustration represent and why is this significant at this point in a Jewish boy's life?

3 Describe the Jewish symbols shown on the illustration and explain their significance.

4 Describe the ceremony and celebrations which take place at a *Bar Mitzvah*.

5 What do you think will be the boy's feelings at this important stage in his life?

6 What responsibilities does the boy now take on?

7 What do you think is the best age for a young person to be recognised as an adult within a community? Give reasons for your opinions.

Rites of Passage

Kiddushin

Activities

 **A** Look in newspapers and magazines for any photographs of weddings taking place in a synagogue. What do you notice about when they take place?

 **B** If you have the *Lifetime of a Jew* wallet available, examine the three documents in it which are connected with marriage: the certificate of marriage, the marriage document and the *ketubah*.

 **C** Discuss the significance of these documents.

 **D** Listen to some of the music from the wedding scene in *Fiddler on the Roof,* if you have the record available.

 **E** Coursework: Compare Jewish marriage customs with those in other religions that you know about. Discuss whether a religious ceremony is likely to make a marriage more stable.

 **F** Attend a Jewish wedding if it is at all possible to do so.

 **G** Complete Worksheet W29, Question with stimulus material on Marriage.

 **H** Make a model of, or an actual *chuppah*.

 **I** 'Blessed art Thou, O Lord our God, who sanctified thy people Israel by the rite of the canopy and the sacred covenant of wedlock.' Answer the following questions:

1 Who will pronounce these words at a Jewish wedding?

2 What is 'the rite of the canopy'?

3 What is meant by the word 'sanctified'?

4 In what way is marriage seen as a sacred covenant?

5 Can you see any advantages of a religious marriage ceremony over a registry office ceremony?

Question with stimulus material on Marriage

Answer the following questions in your file:

1 What is the name of the canopy?

2 What does the canopy symbolise?

3 On which finger(s) of the bride's hand might the ring be placed and why?

4 What are the main points of a *ketubah*?

5 Why is a Jewish marriage called *kiddushin*?

6 In what ways is the importance of marriage and family life stressed in Judaism?

7 What do you think is the meaning of the sentence from the Talmud: 'If a man divorces his first wife, the very altar weeps'?

Rites of Passage

Death

Activities

 **A** Explore a local cemetery if you happen to live in a town with a Jewish community. Make a note of the inscriptions on Jewish tombstones. What do they suggest about Jewish beliefs concerning life after death?

 **B** Research: Discover all you can about Jewish funeral customs and how these reflect beliefs about the nature of God, the nature of man and life after death.

 **C** If you live in an area where there is a Jewish community look for notices of deaths in local newspapers where a Jew may be involved. Do you notice anything about the timing of the funeral?

 **D** Discuss: At the time of a bereavement, is it best to be brave or to give expression to grief? Which is the Jewish practice?

 **E** Complete Worksheet W30, Question with stimulus material on Jewish Mourning Customs.

 **F** Essay on all rites of passage: Attempt all sections of this essay.

1 Give a brief description of what would happen in a synagogue at either a *Bar Mitzvah* or a *Kiddushin*.

2 What is the religious significance of the ceremony that you have chosen?

3 What part does a woman play in Jewish religious observances? Do you think that a distinction should be made between men and women in religious life?

 **G** Revise the work you have done on rites of passage. Test yourself by briefly explaining each of these words:

1 *Bar Mitzvah*   **10** *mitzvot*
2 *Bat Mitzvah*   **11** *mohel*
3 *Bet Hayyim*   **12** *sandek*
4 *Brit Milah*   **13** *Shema*
5 *chuppah*   **14** *shivah*
6 *cohen*   **15** *tallith*
7 *ketubah*   **16** *tephillin*
8 *Kiddushin*   **17** *Yahrzeit*
9 *minyan*   **18** *yarmulke*.

 **H** Look through all the books you have to find photographs of any of the rites of passage. Check that you understand what is happening in the photograph.

Question with stimulus material on Jewish Mourning Customs

Answer the following questions in your file:

1 Why has the coat in the illustration been torn?

2 Describe other Jewish funeral customs.

3 How do these customs help Jews to come to terms with a bereavement?

4 How do Jewish funeral customs reflect their beliefs about life after death?

5 'This world is like a vestibule before the world to come; prepare yourself in the vestibule that you may enter into the hall.' What do you think is the meaning of these words from the Jewish Book of Daily Prayer?

History

A Survey

Activities

A Complete Worksheet W31, 4000 Years of Jewish History. Revise the events and developments that are already familiar to you.

B Research: Using the above sheet and all the books you have available, fill in the gaps in your knowledge. Make this a group activity and share any information with the other students as you discover it.

C Make sure that you know who each of the following were and what part they played in Jewish history:

Abraham
Isaac
Jacob
Moses
David
Solomon
Isaiah
Jeremiah
Ezekiel
Judas Maccabeus
Herod the Great
Simon Bar Kochba
Hillel
Rabbi Akiba
Rabbi Judah
   Ha-Nasi

Rashi – Rabbi
   Solomon ben
   Isaac
Moses Maimonides
Baal Shem Tov –
   Israel ben Eliezer
Sir Moses
   Montefiore
Theodor Herzl
Chaim Weizmann
Leo Baek
Raphael Hirsch
David Ben Gurion
Golda Meir

D Choose one of the people from activity C who interests you particularly and find out as much as possible about him or her.

E Make sure that you understand what happened in the period known as BCE by briefly answering the following questions:

1 Who is known as 'the father of the Jewish nation'?

2 What promise was given to this man concerning his descendants?

3 Who was given the name 'Israel'?

4 To whom was God's name revealed?

5 What does the word 'Exodus' mean?

6 What important event happened on Mount Sinai?

7 How long did the Israelites wander in the wilderness?

8 Which King of Israel is looked upon as the ideal ruler?

9 Who were the original inhabitants of Jerusalem?

10 Who built the first Temple in Jerusalem?

11 When did synagogues first come into existence?

12 Name two prophets who were important in the history of the Jewish people.

13 Which family revolted against Greek rule in Palestine?

14 Who built a magnificent Temple in Jerusalem?

4000 Years of Jewish History

BCE	Event	Related Developments
*c.*2000	Patriarchs: Abraham, Isaac, Jacob	Circumcision, Israel
*c.*1700–1200	Slavery in Egypt	
*c.*1290	Moses, Exodus	Torah, Decalogue, *Yom Kippur, Pesach, Shavuot*, Sukkot
*c.*1000	David, Solomon	Temple
922	Division of the Kingdom, Judah and Israel	
722	Captivity of Israel in Assyria begins	
586	Nebuchadnezzar – destruction of the Temple	
	Exile of Judah in Babylon	Scribes, Synagogues
520	Cyrus – the return from exile	
	Zerubbabel	Second Temple
	Esther	*Purim*
333	Greek persecution begins	*Diaspora*, Pharisees and Sadducees
167	Maccabean revolts	*Chanukkah*
63	Roman period begins, Herod the Great	Herod's Temple

CE		
30	Death of Jesus	
70	Destruction of Jerusalem by Romans	
73	Siege of Masada	
132–5	Simon Bar-Kochba's rebellion	
200–500	Codification of Talmud	*Midrash, Mishnah*
638–1900	Period of mainly Moslem rule	
700s	Anan Ben-David renounced Talmud	*Karaites*
1000–1187	Crusades	Anti–Semitism
1150	Moses Maimonides	Principles of the Faith
1400s	Inquisition in Spain	*Shephardim*
	Migration into East Europe	*Ashkenazim*, Ghettos
1530–1650	Jewish mysticism, centred on Safed	*Kabbalah*
1657	Jews allowed into England	
1700s	Anti-intellectual movement stressing religious fervour	*Hasidism*
1895	Theodor Herzl 'The Jewish State'	First Zionist Congress
1917	Balfour Declaration, Chaim Weizmann	Zionism
1939–45	Second World War, Nazism	Pogroms, Holocaust
1948	Foundation of the State of Israel	

Do not try to learn the information above. It is for reference!

Answer the following questions in your file:

1 Make a list of events and related developments which you do not understand. Look them up in appropriate textbooks.

2 Trace and make notes on the periods of persecution suffered by Jews down the ages.

History

The State of Israel

Activities

 **A** Complete Worksheet W32, Map of Israel

 **B** Coursework: Collect newspaper items and other media information on current relations between Israel and neighbouring countries. Produce an illustrated assessment of the situation.

 **C** Collect as many illustrations of Israel as you can. (Travel brochures are often useful.) Stick them around a map of Israel or make a collage.

 **D** Sketch the emblem of Israel. Discover what you can about the symbolism of the emblem and annotate your sketch.

 **E** If you know of anyone, perhaps a former student, who has worked on an Israeli kibbutz, invite them to tell you of their experiences.

 **F** Imagine that you are a Russian Jew who has been given permission to emigrate to Israel. What problems are you likely to encounter in your new country?

 **G** Discuss: 'He will assemble the dispersed of Israel and gather together the scattered of Judah from the four corners of the earth' (Isaiah 11:12). What effect has this prophecy had upon the Jewish people?

 **H** Divide into groups of four or five. Imagine that you are a Jewish family and that it has been suggested that you all emigrate to Israel. Role-play the conversation that follows, making sure that both the advantages and the disadvantages are discussed.

 **I** Revise the work you did on the celebration of *Yom ha-Azmaut* (Topic 7k).

J Find out as much as you can about the Balfour Declaration.

Map of Israel

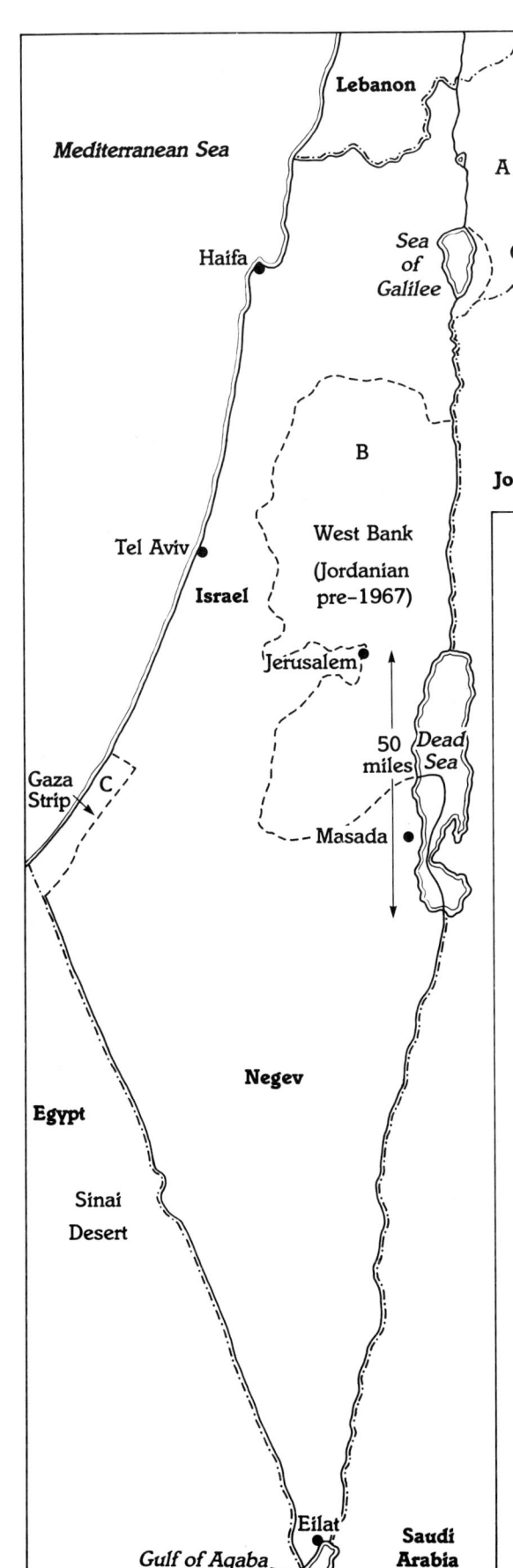

Key

- — · — Present boundary
- — — — Pre-1967 boundary

(NB Golan Heights boundary is pre-1973)

A, B, C   Occupied territories

Answer the following questions in your file:

1 Using a physical map of Israel in an atlas, trace the course of the pre-1967 boundary. Does this follow natural features?

2 What is the approximate distance of Israel's pre-1967 boundaries?

3 How many countries surround Israel?

4 From the information you have discovered, what problems would you expect to find in the area?

5 If the political situation has changed since this map was drawn, draw another map showing the new boundaries.

6 Before 1967 Jerusalem was partitioned between Israel and Jordan. There are suggestions that this should happen again. Make a list of problems which might result from a city such as Jerusalem being divided between two countries.

7 Find out and list the major changes of boundaries which have occurred since 1948.

History

Persecution

Activities

A Watch a video, film or sound-strip of the Holocaust if it is at all possible. (*Ages of Anguish* in the Jewish Tradition series is excellent.)

B Look for any books about the persecution of Jews during this century, for example, *The Diary of Anne Frank*.

C Discuss: A recent article in a provincial newspaper under the heading 'Haunted by the Holocaust' described the efforts of a group of MPs to investigate alleged Nazi war criminals now living in Britain. If such people exist, should charges be brought against them 40 years after the alleged crimes? Share your views.

D Essay: Attempt all sections of this essay.

1 What is anti-Semitism?

2 What name is given to the persecution of the Jews during the Second World War? What is the meaning of the word?

3 What was meant by 'the final solution'?

4 What effects did the persecution have upon the Jews worldwide?

5 It has been suggested that it would be better to forget about the persecution of the Jews, as the events were so horrific. Another point of view was expressed by former Prime Minister, David Ben Gurion, who said 'Forgive, but never forget.' What is your opinion?

E Complete Worksheet W33, Question with stimulus material on the State of Israel.

F Revise the work you did about *Yom ha-Shoah* (Topic 7k).

G The Hebrew word *shoah* literally means 'whirlwind'. Discuss: Is this an effective description of the Holocaust?

H Revise the work you did on the periods of persecution suffered by Jews (Topic 9a, Worksheet W31).

Question with stimulus material on the State of Israel

Answer the following questions in your file:

1 What is the symbol in the centre of the flag of Israel?

2 What are the colours of the flag and what is their significance?

3 What do you understand by the term Zionism? What problems has the Zionist movement given rise to?

4 What is (a) a *moshav* and (b) a kibbutz? Why were these two systems set up? Suggest some contributions that they have made to the State.

5 Some Jewish communities have added a new day of commemoration to the Jewish calendar – *Yom ha-Shoah,* in commemoration of the Holocaust. Do you think this is a good idea? Give your reasons.

Pilgrimage

Activities

 **A** Find travel brochures on the Middle East and collect photographs of Jerusalem. Make a collage or display the photographs attractively.

 **B** Research: Use all the books you have available to discover why the following locations are places of pilgrimage for Jews:

1 The Western Wall
2 Yad Vashem
3 Masada.

 **C** Discuss: When the Western Wall was recaptured in 1967, General Moshe Dayan said, 'We have come back to our holiest of holy places, never to be parted from it again.' Then, following an ancient practice, he wrote a prayer which was left in a crack in the wall. The prayer was 'Let peace reign in Israel.'

1 What political and religious implications do you see in General Dayan's words?

2 What prayer might you leave there?

 **D** Watch part of the TV series *Masada*, if you have access to a video. Discuss the Jewish slogan 'Masada shall not fall again'.

 **E** Coursework: You have met a group of Jewish young people who have recently returned from a visit to Israel. Write an illustrated account of the places they visited and their feelings about the pilgrimage.

 **F** If you know of anyone who has recently visited Israel, invite them to show slides or describe the places mentioned in activity B.

 **G** Complete Worksheet W34, Question with stimulus material on Pilgrimage.

 **H** Describe three important objects you would see at Yad Vashem and explain their significance.

 **I** New recruits to the armoured units of Israel's forces swear their oath of allegiance on top of the fortress of Masada. Discuss why this location is very significant for them.

Question with stimulus material on Pilgrimage

Answer the following questions in your file:

1 What is this structure and where is it?

2 What are these Jews doing here?

3 Why is this such an important place of pilgrimage for Jews?

4 Name two other places of pilgrimage for Jews.

5 Explain why one of the two places of pilgrimage is visited by Jews.

6 Do you think that it is important that a religion should have holy places that are visited by pilgrims?

7 Could you make any suggestions for appropriate prayers to be offered at this spot?

Revision

Activities

 **A** Complete the test on Worksheet W35.

 **B** Complete the wordsearch on Worksheet W36.

 **C** Discuss the following statements about Judaism or attempt essays on some of the subjects:

1 Judaism is a religion, but it is also the historical experience of the Jewish people.

2 The existence of the Jews is the best proof of the existence of God.

3 At the heart of Judaism lies unbounded optimism.

4 The most highly prized possession of the Jewish religion is the Torah.

5 Many of the most important acts of Jewish worship are carried out in the home with parents and children participating.

6 It is not the function of the rabbi to conduct synagogue services.

7 Nature and natural events play an important part in Jewish religious practice.

8 The practices of Judaism on festival days emphasise the historical foundation of its religious beliefs and actions.

9 The Jews have survived without synagogues but they could not survive without families.

10 The effects of persecution upon the Jewish people have been positive as well as negative.

11 Israel is that unprecedented act of reconstruction which followed the unprecedented act of destruction.

 **D** Prayer is tremendously important to Jews. Revise all the blessings (*berakhot*) that you have discovered during the course and also the occasions on which they are used.

 **E** Look through the scrapbook that you started in Topic 2. Make sure that you understand the significance of everything that you have included.

 **F** The Talmud suggests that there are four types of student:

1 The sponge which absorbs and retains everything.

2 The funnel where everything that goes in comes out.

3 The sifter which remembers the trivial and forgets the significant.

4 The sieve which retains the important and sifts out the incidental. Which of these types of student are you?

 **G** Revise all your work before the examination, and every success with it!

Mazal Tov!

Test

Write a sentence to explain the meaning of each of the following words:

1 Synagogue _____

2 Torah _____

3 *Bimah* _____

4 *Pesach* _____

5 *Bar Mitzvah* _____

6 *Mezuzah* _____

7 *Purim* _____

8 *Menorah* _____

9 *Shema* _____

10 *Challah* _____

11 Kosher _____

12 *Hazzan* _____

13 *Tephillin* _____

14 *Amidah* _____

15 *Havdalah* _____

16 *Rosh Hashanah* _____

17 *Haroseth* _____

18 *Shavuot* _____

19 *Kiddushin* _____

20 *Chanukkah* _____

21 *Haggadah* _____

22 *Simchat Torah* _____

23 *Tallith* _____

24 Talmud _____

25 *Ketubah* _____

26 *Yom Kippur* _____

27 *Shofar* _____

28 *Yarmulka* _____

29 *Sukkot* _____

30 *Seder* _____

A Wordsearch on Judaism

```
R  T  E  P  H  I  L  L  I  N  O  K
Y  O  M  K  I  P  P  U  R  I  I  O
A  R  S  H  O  F  A  R  A  D  V  A
D  A  H  H  A  M  A  N  D  I  R  Z
H  H  A  C  H  A  N  U  K  K  A  H
A  S  V  S  O  A  S  H  E  M  A  N
Z  E  U  C  D  H  S  M  I  R  U  P
U  D  O  K  I  N  B  H  B  I  G  E
Z  E  T  N  K  M  R  E  A  G  E  S
E  R  O  G  T  O  I  U  R  N  M  A
M  D  U  M  L  A  T  G  M  E  A  C
I  B  B  A  R  E  M  O  I  V  R  H
V  A  S  L  N  A  I  G  T  I  A  A
U  S  U  A  T  K  L  A  Z  I  A  M
T  L  K  Z  E  O  A  N  V  M  D  I
E  H  O  A  R  O  H  Y  A  V  A  B
K  S  I  L  M  K  O  S  H  E  R  E
```

List below the 32 Hebrew words hidden above. The first has been done for you:

Adar

_____ _____ _____

_____ _____ _____

_____ _____ _____

_____ _____ _____

_____ _____ _____

_____ _____ _____

_____ _____ _____

_____ _____ _____

_____ _____ _____

_____ _____ _____

_____